SELECTED POEMS OF RŪMĪ

DOVER THRIFT EDITIONS

Jalālu'l-Dīn Rūmī

Translated from the Persian
with Introduction and Notes by

Reynold A. Nicholson

DOVER PUBLICATIONS
GARDEN CITY, NEW YORK

Copyright

Bibliographical Note

This Dover edition, first published in 2001 and reissued in 2011, is an unabridged republication of the work originally published as Number I in the series, "Ethical and Religious Classics of the East and West," by George Allen and Unwin Ltd., London, in 1950 under the title *Rūmī: Poet and Mystic (1207–1273)*. The general introduction to the series has been omitted.

Library of Congress Cataloging-in-Publication Data

Jalal al-Din Rumi, Maulana, 1207–1273.
[Poems. English. Selections]
Selected poems of Rumi / Jalalu'l-Din Rumi ; translated from the Persian with introduction and notes by Reynold A. Nicholson.
p. cm. — (Dover thrift editions)
Originally published: Rumi, poet and mystic, 1207–1273. London : George Allen and Unwin, 1950. (Ethical and religious classics of the East and West ; no. 1)
ISBN-13: 978-0-486-41583-3
ISBN-10: 0-486-41583-X
1. Jalâl al-Dân Râmâ, Maulana, 1207–1273—Translations into English. 2. Sufi poetry, Persian—Translations into English. I. Nicholson, Reynold Alleyne, 1868–1945. II. Title. III. Series.

PK6480.E5 N5 2001
891'.5511—dc21

00-052302

Manufactured in the United States by LSC Communications Book LLC
41583X14 2021
www.doverpublications.com

Preface

WHEN Professor R. A. Nicholson died in August 1945, he left behind him the manuscript of "a book of translations illustrating Ṣūfī doctrine and experience as depicted by the greatest of Iranian mystical poets, Jalālu'l-Dīn Rūmī." The main text of the book was complete, but the introduction was unfinished. It has fallen to me to see this work through the press. In discharging this proud obligation of piety to my teacher and dearest friend I have redrafted into the present introduction most of the materials he prepared, allowing myself no liberty of personal opinion except in the two concluding paragraphs.

1950 A. J. ARBERRY

Contents

INTRODUCTION

I

Jalālu'l-Dīn Rūmī, the greatest mystical poet of Persia, was born at Balkh in the northern Persian province of Khorasan in A.D. 1207. The city at that time flourished under the rule of Muḥammad, the great Shah of Khwarizm, whose empire, as E. G. Browne described it, "extended from the Ural Mountains to the Persian Gulf, and from the Indus almost to the Euphrates." The family to which our poet belonged had been settled in Balkh for several generations; it was highly respected and, according to his biographers, had produced a notable succession of jurists and divines. So far as can be ascertained, its history begins with his great-grandfather, who claimed descent from Arab stock, and from no less a person than Abū Bakr, the first Caliph of Islam.

Although the Eastern biographies of Rūmī, like other lives of Persian saints, are to a large extent legendary, while his own works characteristically contribute virtually nothing in the shape of historical facts, we are fortunate in possessing some old and relatively trustworthy sources of information.[1] The following sketch, based on the chief materials available, gives briefly the main circumstances of Rūmī's life and describes some of the events which were the source of his mystical enthusiasm and poetic inspiration.

In 1219, when Jalālu'l-Dīn was twelve years old, his father, Bahā'u'l-Dīn Walad, suddenly departed from Balkh with his family and journeyed westward. The motives alleged for this migration, that it was the result either of divine inspiration or human intrigue, are surely fictitious. There can be no doubt that Bahā'u'l-Dīn, like many thousands of others, fled before the terrible Mongol hordes, which were sweeping

[1] See Note, p. xix.

through Khorasan and already approaching his native city. News of its devastation reached the exiles on their way to Baghdad or on the next stage of their long journey from Baghdad to Mecca, when they travelled to Damascus and finally settled in Rum (Turkey).

Their first home was at Zarandah, about forty miles south-east of Konia, where Jalālu'l-Dīn married; in 1226 his eldest son Sultān Walad was born. Presently Bahā'u'l-Dīn transferred himself and his family to Konia, at that time the capital of the Western Seljuk empire, and he died there in 1230. He is said to have been an eminent theologian, a great teacher and preacher, venerated by his pupils and highly esteemed by the reigning monarch, to whom he acted as a spiritual guide. About this time Burhānu'l-Dīn Muḥaqqiq of Tirmidh, a former pupil of Bahā'u'l-Dīn at Balkh, arrived in Konia. Under his influence, it is said, Jalālu'l-Dīn, now in his twenty-fifth year, became imbued with enthusiasm for the discipline and doctrine of the Ṣūfīs—men and women who sought to unite themselves with God. During the next decade he devoted himself to imitation of his Pīr and passed through all the stages of the mystical life until, on the death of Burhānu'l-Dīn in 1240, he in turn assumed the rank of Shaykh and thus took the first, though probably unpremeditated, step towards forming a fraternity of the disciples whom his ardent personality attracted in ever increasing numbers.

The remainder of his life, as described by his son, falls into three periods, each of which is marked by a mystical intimacy of the closest kind with a "Perfect Man," i.e. one of the saints in whom Divine attributes are mirrored, so that the lover, seeing himself by the light of God, realizes that he and his Beloved are not two, but One. These experiences lie at the very centre of Rūmī's theosophy and directly or indirectly inspire all his poetry. In handling the verse narrative of a mystic's son who was himself a mystic it is prudent to make ample allowance for the element of allegory; yet it would be rash to reject the whole story as pious fiction seeing that at the date when it was written many persons were living who could say whether it was, or was not, a recognizable picture of things which they themselves had witnessed.

In 1244 a wandering dervish, known to posterity by the name of Shamsu'l-Dīn of Tabriz, arrived at Konia. Jalālu'l-Dīn found in the stranger that perfect image of the Divine Beloved which he had long been seeking. He took him away to his house, and for a year or two they remained inseparable. Sulṭān Walad likens his father's all-absorbing communion with this "hidden saint" to the celebrated journey of Moses in company with Khaḍir (Koran, xviii, 64–80), the Sage whom Ṣūfīs regard as the supreme hierophant and guide of travellers on the

Way to God. Meanwhile the Maulawī (Mevlevi)[2] disciples of Rūmī, entirely cut off from their Master's teaching and conversation and bitterly resenting his continued devotion to Shamsu'l-Dīn alone, assailed the intruder with abuse and threats of violence. At last Shamsu'l-Dīn fled to Damascus, but was brought back in triumph by Sulṭān Walad, whom Jalālu'l-Dīn, deeply agitated by the loss of his bosom friend, had sent in search of him. Thereupon the disciples "repented" and were forgiven. Soon, however, a renewed outburst of jealousy on their part caused Shamsu'l-Dīn to take refuge in Damascus for the second time, and again Sulṭān Walad was called upon to restore the situation. Finally, perhaps in 1247, the man of mystery vanished without leaving a trace behind.

Sulṭān Walad vividly describes the passionate and uncontrollable emotion which overwhelmed his father at this time.

> "Never for a moment did he cease from listening to music (*samā'*), and dancing;
> Never did he rest by day or night.
> He had been a mufti: he became a poet;
> He had been an ascetic: he became intoxicated by Love.
> 'Twas not the wine of the grape: the illumined soul drinks only the wine of Light."

Here Sulṭān Walad alludes to the *Dīwān-i Shams-i Tabrīz* ("Lyrics of Shams of Tabriz"), an immense collection of mystical odes composed by Jalālu'l-Dīn in the name of Shamsu'l-Dīn and dedicated to the memory of his *alter ego*. The first verse does not confirm, but may have suggested, the statement of some authorities that grief for the loss of Shams-i Tabrīz caused Jalālu'l-Dīn to institute the characteristic Mevlevi religious dance with its plaintive reed-flute accompaniment.

The next episode (*circa* 1252–1261) in Jalālu'l-Dīn's spiritual life is a fainter repetition of the last. For many years after the disappearance of Shamsu'l-Dīn he devoted himself to Ṣalāḥu'l-Dīn Farīdūn Zarkūb, who as his deputy (*khalīfah*) was charged with the duty of instructing the Mevlevi acolytes. They showed their resentment in no uncertain manner, and the ringleaders only gave in when they had been virtually excommunicated.

On the death of Ṣalāḥu'l-Dīn (*circa* 1261) the poet's enthusiasm found a new and abundant source of inspiration in another disciple, Ḥusāmu'l-Dīn Ḥasan ibn Muḥammad ibn Ḥasan ibn Akhī Turk, whose name he has mystically associated with his greatest work, the

[2] The title for Rūmī's followers; Rūmī was known among them as *Maulānā* ("Our Master"). Mevlevi is the Turkish pronunciation of Maulawī.

celebrated *Mathnawī* (epic poem). He calls the *Mathnawī* "the book of Ḥusām" and likens himself to a flute on the lips of Ḥusāmu'l-Dīn, pouring forth "the wailful music that he made." During the last ten years of the poet's life this last beloved follower acted as his *khalīfah*, and upon his death in 1273 succeeded him as Head of the Mevlevi Order, a dignity he held until 1284, when Sulṭān Walad took his place.

To this first-hand account of Rūmī's life given in verse by his son the later prose biographers add little that can be considered either important or trustworthy. From Aflākī and others we hear that he was guide, philosopher and friend, not only to the Seljuk minister Mu'īnu'l-Dīn, the Parwānah (Governor) of Rum, but to his royal master, Sulṭān 'Alā'u'l-Dīn himself; in any case it would seem that he and the group of Ṣūfīs around him enjoyed influential support and were in a position to defy attacks on their doctrine. The poet takes a high line with his orthodox critics. He calls them "boobies" and "curs baying at the moon."

A Platonic type of mystical love had been cultivated by Ṣūfīs long before Rūmī declared that he and Shams-i Tabrīz were "two bodies with one soul." In this union of loving souls all distinctions vanish: nothing remains but the essential Unity of Love, in which "lover" and "beloved" have merged their separate identities. In calling his lyrics the *Dīwān* (Poems) of Shams-i Tabrīz, Rūmī of course uses the name Shams as though Shams and himself had become identical and were the same person. Though to us Shams's figure may appear unsubstantial, we need not accept the view put forward by some modern scholars that he is merely a personification of Jalālu'l-Dīn's poetic and mystical genius—an Eastern equivalent for "the Muse." Those who adopt that theory must logically extend it to include Ṣalāḥu'l-Dīn and Ḥusāmu'l-Dīn and can hardly avoid the implication that Sulṭān Walad created three imaginary characters to play the leading parts in his father's life and in the foundation of the Mevlevi Order. Western students of the *Dīwān* and the *Mathnawī* will recall a celebrated parallel that points the other way. Did not Dante transfigure the *donna gentil* who was the object of his romantic passion into Celestial Wisdom and glorify her under the name of Beatrice?

II

Rūmī's literary output, as stupendous in magnitude as it is sublime in content, consists of the very large collection of mystical odes, perhaps as many as 2,500, which make up the *Dīwān-i Shams-i Tabrīz*; the *Mathnawī* in six books of about 25,000 rhyming couplets; and the *Rubā'īyat* or quatrains, of which maybe about 1,600 are authentic.[3] The forms in which he clothes his religious philosophy had been fashioned before him by two great Ṣūfī poets, Sanā'ī of Ghaznah and Farīdu'l-Dīn 'Aṭṭār of Nishapur. Though he makes no secret of his debt to them both, his flight takes a wider range, his materials are richer and more varied, and his method of handling the subject is so original that it may justly be described as "a new style." It is a style of great subtlety and complexity, hard to analyse; yet its general features are simple and cannot be doubted. In the *Mathnawī*, where it is fully developed, it gives the reader an exhilarating sense of largeness and freedom by its disregard for logical cohesion, defiance of conventions, bold use of the language of common life, and abundance of images drawn from homely things and incidents familiar to every one. The poem resembles a trackless ocean: there are no boundaries; no lines of demarcation between the literal "husk" and the "kernel" of doctrine in which its inner sense is conveyed and copiously expounded. The effortless fusion of text and interpretation shows how completely, in aesthetics as in every other domain, the philosophy of Rūmī is inspired by the monistic idea. "The *Mathnawī*," he says, "is the shop for Unity (*waḥdat*); anything that you see there except the One (God) is an idol." Ranging over the battlefield of existence, he finds all its conflicts and discords playing the parts assigned to them in the universal harmony which only mystics can realize.

Ṣūfī pantheism or monism involves the following propositions:

(*a*) There is One Real Being, the Ultimate Ground of all existence. This Reality may be viewed either as God (the Divine Essence) or as the World (phenomena by which the hidden Essence is made manifest).

(*b*) There is no creation in Time. Divine Self-manifestation is a perpetual process. While the *forms* of the universe change and pass and are simultaneously renewed without a moment's intermission, in its *essence* it is co-eternal with God. There never was a time when it did not exist as a whole in His Knowledge.

(*c*) God is both Immanent, in the sense that He appears under the aspect of limitation in all phenomenal forms, and Transcendent, in the sense that He is the Absolute Reality above and beyond every appearance.

(*d*) The Divine Essence is unknowable. God makes His Nature known to us by Names and Attributes which He has revealed in the Koran. Though essentially identical, from our point of view the Divine Attributes are diverse and opposed to each other, and this

---

[3][This sentence has been added to the author's draft.—A. J. A.]

differentiation constitutes the phenomenal world, without which we could not distinguish good from evil and come to know the Absolute Good. In the sphere of Reality there is no such thing as evil.

(*e*) According to the Holy Tradition, "I created the creatures in order than I might be known," the entire content of God's Knowledge is objectified in the universe and pre-eminently in Man. The Divine Mind, which rules and animates the cosmos as an Indwelling Rational Principle (Logos), displays itself completely in the Perfect Man. The supreme type of the Perfect Man is the pre-existent Reality or Spirit of Muḥammad, whose "Light" irradiates the long series of prophets beginning with Adam and, after them, the hierarchy of Muslim saints, who are Muḥammad's spiritual heirs. Whether prophet or saint, the Perfect Man has realized his Oneness with God: he is the authentic image and manifestation of God and therefore the final cause of creation, since only through him does God become fully conscious of Himself.

These are some of the themes underlying Rūmī's poetry. He is not their original author; they may be regarded as having been gradually evolved by the long succession of Ṣūfī thinkers from the ninth century onwards, then gathered together and finally formulated by the famous Andalusian mystic, Ibnu'l-'Arabī (1165–1240). Ibnu'l-'Arabī has every right to be called the father of Islamic pantheism. He devoted colossal powers of intellect and imagination to constructing a system which, though it lacks order and connexion, covers the whole ground in detail and perhaps, all things considered, is the most imposing monument of mystical speculation the world has ever seen. While it is evident that Rūmī borrowed some part of his terminology and ideas from his elder contemporary, who himself travelled in Rum and lies buried in Damascus, the amount of the debt has inevitably been exaggerated by later commentators whose minds are filled with forms of thought alien to the *Mathnawī* but familiar to readers of Ibnu'l-'Arabī's *Fuṣūṣu'l-ḥikam* ("Bezels of Wisdom") and *al-Futūḥātu'l-Makkiyya* ("Meccan Revelations"). The Andalusian always writes with a fixed *philosophical* purpose, which may be defined as the *logical* development of a single all-embracing concept, and much of his thought expresses itself in a dialectic bristling with technicalities. Rūmī has no such aim. As E. H. Whinfield said, his mysticism is not "doctrinal" in the Catholic sense but "experimental." He appeals to the heart more than to the head, scorns the logic of the schools, and nowhere does he embody in philosophical language even the elements of a system. The words used by Dante in reference to the *Divine Commedia* would serve excellently as a description of the *Mathnawī*: "the poem belongs to the moral or ethical branch of philosophy, its quality is not speculative but practical, and its ultimate end is to lead into the state of felicity those now enduring the miserable life of man." The *Mathnawī* for the most part shows Rūmī as the perfect spiritual guide engaged in making others perfect and furnishing novice and adept alike with matter suitable to their needs. Assuming the general monistic theory to be well known to his readers, he gives them a panoramic view of the Ṣūfī gnosis (direct intuition of God) and kindles their enthusiasm by depicting the rapture of those who "break through to the Oneness" and see all mysteries revealed.[4]

While the *Mathnawī* is generally instructional in character, though it also has entertaining passages, as befits a book intended for the enlightenment of all sorts of disciples, the *Dīwān* and, on a much smaller scale, the *Rubā'īyāt* are personal and emotional in appeal. Lyrics and quatrains alike have everywhere the authentic ring of spiritual inspiration, while in image, style and language they often approximate very closely to the *Mathnawī*. In some of these poems the mystic's passion is so exuberant, his imagination so overflowing, that we catch glimpses of the very madness of Divine experience. Yet the powerful intellect of Rūmī the man never quite capitulates to the enthusiasm of Rūmī the mystic; at the last moment there is a sudden drawing-back, a consciousness that certain matters are too secret and too holy to be communicated in words. It is not surprising to read that these poems, chanted (as many of them were doubtless composed) in the spiritual séance of the Mevlevis, roused the hearers to an almost uncontrollable fervour.

In Rūmī the Persian mystical genius found its supreme expression. Viewing the vast landscape of Ṣūfī poetry, we see him standing out as a sublime mountain-peak; the many other poets before and after him are but foot-hills in comparison. The influence of his example, his thought and his language is powerfully felt through all the succeeding centuries; every Ṣūfī after him capable of reading Persian has acknowledged his unchallenged leadership. To the West, now slowly realizing the magnitude of his genius, thanks in greatest measure to the work of that fine scholar whose last writings are contained in these pages, he is fully able to prove a source of inspiration and delight not surpassed by any other poet in the world's literature.

---

[4]Here Professor Nicholson's notes end.

APPENDIX

NOTE

MOST interesting of the biographical materials on Rūmī is the *Ibtidā-nāmah* ("Book of Beginning") a long narrative poem composed by Rūmī's son Sulṭān Walad; valuable information is also contained in the *Manāqibu'l-'ārifin* ("Virtues of the Gnostics") of Aflākī, disciple of the poet's grandson Chelebī 'Ārif, which C. Huart translated as *Les Saints des derviches tourneurs* (Paris, 1918–22). In addition we have a number of books, like the *Fīhi mā fīhi* ("In it what is In it") (published at Teheran and Azamgarh in 1928) and the *Maqālāt-i Shams-i Tabrīz* ("Discourses of Shams-i Tabrīz") (still unedited), which, though shedding little light upon the life, go far to illuminate the ideas and doctrines of the poet.

In modern times the Persian scholar Badī'u'l-Zamān Furūzānfarr has written a valuable critical study of Rūmī's life [*Sharḥ-i ḥāl-i Maulānā* ("Biography of our Master"), Teheran 1932], and the learned Dr. H. Ritter has contributed a bio-bibliographical review of the whole subject (in *Der Islam*, 1940, 1942) which is as masterly as it is indispensable to any interested in this field of research.

PRELUDE[1]

Deep in our hearts the Light of Heaven is shining
  Upon a soundless Sea without a shore.
Oh, happy they who found it in resigning
  The images of all that men adore.

Blind eyes, to dote on shadows of things fair
  Only at last to curse their fatal lure,
Like Harut and Marut, that Angel-pair
  Who deemed themselves the purest of the pure.

Our ignorance and self-will and vicious pride
  Destroy the harmony of part and whole.
In vain we seek with lusts unmor tified
  A vision of the One Eternal Soul.

Love, Love alone can kill what seemed so dead,
  The frozen snake[2] of passion. Love alone,
By tearful prayer and fiery longing fed,
  Reveals a knowledge schools have never known.

God's lovers learn from Him the secret ways
  Of Providence, the universal plan.
Living in Him, they ever sing His praise
  Who made the myriad worlds of Time for Man.

---

[1]This is not a translation—it has no original text behind it. I wrote to please myself, but seeing that it brings together some of Rūmī's characteristic ideas in a simple and compendious form, I think it may well serve as an overture to the present work.

[2]The "frozen snake," or dragon, which symbolizes the carnal soul, is never so dangerous as when it pretends to have been utterly subdued and crushed. In the *Mathnawī* Rūmī relates how a hunter discovered this monstrous creature half buried in snow. To all appearance it had been killed by the intense frost. He conveyed it to Baghdad, opened a public show, and announced that on payment of a small fee it might be viewed by any one whose curiosity it excited. Spectators came in crowds, but now the season had changed. Reviving under the fierce heat of a Mesopotamian summer, the dragon began to uncoil. The ensuing havoc and slaughter were terrible to see.

Evil they knew not, for in Him there's none;
Yet without evil how should good be seen?
Love answers: "Feel with me, with me be one;
Where I am, naught stands up to come between."

There are degrees of Heavenly Light in souls:
Prophets and Saints have shown the Path they trod,
Its starting points and stages, halts and goals,
All leading to the single end in God.

Love will not let his faithful servants tire,
Immortal Beauty draws them on and on
From glory unto glory, drawing nigher
At each remove and loving to be drawn.

When Truth shines out words fail and nothing tell;
Now hear the Voice within your hearts. Farewell.

I.
THE SONG OF THE REED[1]

Hearken to this Reed forlorn,
Breathing, even since 'twas torn
From its rushy bed, a strain
Of impassioned love and pain.

"The secret of my song, though near,
None can see and none can hear.
Oh, for a friend to know the sign[2]
And mingle all his soul with mine!

'Tis the flame of Love that fired me,
'Tis the wine of Love inspired me.
Wouldst thou learn how lovers bleed,
Hearken, hearken to the Reed!"

[1]*Math.* I, 1. The opening lines of the poem strike a keynote that recurs insistently throughout. The Persian reed-flute (*nay*) has always been associated with the religious services of the Maulawī Order, in which music and dancing are prominent features. Rūmī uses it as a symbol for the soul emptied of self and filled with the Divine spirit. This blessed soul, during its life on earth, remembers the union with God which it enjoyed in eternity and longs ardently for deliverance from the world where it is a stranger and exile.

[2]*i.e.* a soul of its own kind. Only the mystic understands the mystic.

II.
REMEMBERED MUSIC[1]

'Tis said, the pipe and lute that charm our ears
Derive their melody from rolling spheres;[2]
But Faith, o'erpassing speculation's bound,
Can see what sweetens every jangled sound.[3]

We, who are parts of Adam, heard with him
The song of angels and of seraphim.
Our memory, though dull and sad, retains
Some echo still of those unearthly strains.

Oh, music is the meat of all who love,
Music uplifts the soul to realms above.
The ashes glow, the latent fires increase:
We listen and are fed with joy and peace.

III.
LOVE IN ABSENCE[1]

How should not I mourn, like night, without His day and the favour of His day-illuming countenance?
His unsweetness is sweet to my soul: may my soul be sacrificed to the Beloved who grieves my heart!
I am in love with grief and pain for the sake of pleasing my peerless King.
Tears shed for His sake are pearls, though people think they are tears.

---

[1]*Math.* IV, 733.

[2]The well-known theory of Pythagoras is almost a commonplace in Moslem philosophy and poetry. According to the Pure Brethren (*Ikhwānu 'l-ṣafā*) of Basra, "since the celestial spheres revolve and the planets and stars are moved, it follows that they must have musical notes and expressions with which God is glorified, delighting the souls of the angels, just as in the corporeal world our souls listen with delight to melodies and obtain relief from care and sorrow. And inasmuch as these melodies are but echoes of heavenly music, they recall to us the spacious gardens of Paradise and the pleasures enjoyed by the souls dwelling there; and then our souls long to fly up thither and rejoin their mates."

[3]Ṣūfīs associate the spiritual influence of music with the pre-existence of the soul. While listening, they hear again the Voice of God to which all human souls responded in eternity (*Qur'ān* VII, 171) and the anthems of the Heavenly Host.

---

[1]*Math.* I, 1776.

I complain of the Soul of my soul, but in truth I am not complaining: I am only telling.[2]
My heart says it is tormented by Him, and I have long been laughing at its poor pretence.[3]
Do me right, O Glory of the righteous, O Thou Who art the dais, and I the threshold of Thy door!
Where are threshold and dais in reality? Where the Beloved is, where are "we" and "I"?
O Thou Whose soul is free from "we" and "I", O Thou Who art the essence of the spirit in men and women,
When men and women become one, Thou art that One; when the units are wiped out, lo, Thou art that Unity.[4]
Thou didst contrive this "I" and "we" in order to play the game of worship with Thyself,[5]
That all "I's" and "thou's" might become one soul and at last be submerged in the Beloved.

IV.
"THE MARRIAGE OF TRUE MINDS"[1]

Happy the moment when we are seated in the palace, thou and I,
With two forms and with two figures but with one soul, thou and I.
The colours of the grove and the voices of the birds will bestow immortality
At the time when we shall come into the garden, thou and I.
The stars of Heaven will come to gaze upon us:
We shall show them the moon herself, thou and I.
Thou and I, individuals no more, shall be mingled in ecstasy,
Joyful and secure from foolish babble, thou and I.

---

[2]While self-conscious lovers complain of separation from the beloved one and reproach her for her cruelty, the mystic's complaint (*shikāyat*) is really no more than the tale (*ḥikāyat*) of his infinite longing for God—a tale which God inspires him to tell.
[3]*i.e.* "I know that my anguish is a token of God's Loving-kindness."
[4]All phenomena are individualized modes of Real Being; when stripped of their individuality, they become one with each other and with Real Being. Hence God reveals Himself in every union of loving souls.
[5]Essentially God is both the Object of worship and the worshipper. The illusion of individuality—"I" and "we"—arises from the interplay of two opposite aspects, essence and form, under which the One Reality may be regarded.

---

[1]*Dīwān, S. P.*, XXXVIII. A description of mystical union, in which the antithesis of "lover" and "beloved" is resolved by their transmutation into the Universal Essence of Love.

All the bright-plumed birds of Heaven will devour their hearts with envy
In the place where we shall laugh in such a fashion, thou and I.
This is the greatest wonder, that thou and I, sitting here in the same nook,
Are at this moment both in 'Irāq and Khorāsān, thou and I.

V.
"A SLEEP AND A FORGETTING"[1]

One who has lived many years in a city, so soon as he goes to sleep,
Beholds another city full of good and evil, and his own city vanishes from his mind.
He does not say to himself, "This is a new city: I am a stranger here";
Nay, he thinks he has always lived in this city and was born and bred in it.
What wonder, then, if the soul does not remember her ancient abode and birth-place,
Since she is wrapt in the slumber of this world, like a star covered by clouds?—
Especially as she has trodden so many cities and the dust that darkens her vision is not yet swept away.[2]

VI.
THE GRIEF OF THE DEAD[1]

The Prince of mankind (Mohammed) said truly that no one who has passed away from this world
Feels sorrow and regret for having died; nay, but he feels a hundred regrets for having missed the opportunity,
Saying to himself, "Why did I not make death my object—death which is the store-house of all fortunes and riches,[2]
And why, through seeing double, did I fasten my lifelong gaze upon those phantoms that vanished at the fated hour?"
The grief of the dead is not on account of death; it is because they dwelt on the phenomenal forms of existence

---

[1]*Math.* IV, 3628.
[2]See No. CXVIII. The "cities" are the planes of being or phases of experience traversed by the soul in its journeys *from* and *to* God, *i.e.* its descent from the real to the phenomenal world and its subsequent return from plurality to Unity.

---

[1]*Math.* VI, 1450. Cf. No. XXVII.
[2]Here "death" signifies "dying to self" (*fanā*). Cf. the Prophet's saying, "Die before ye die."

And never perceived that all this foam is moved and fed by the Sea.[3]
When the Sea has cast the foam-flakes on the shore, go to the graveyard and behold them!
Say to them, "Where is your swirling onrush now?" and hear them answer mutely, "Ask this question of the Sea, not of us."
How should the foam fly without the wave? How should the dust rise to the zenith without the wind?
Since you have seen the dust, see the Wind; since you have seen the foam, see the Ocean of Creative Energy.
Come, see it, for insight is the only thing in you that avails: the rest of you is a piece of fat and flesh, a woof and warp (of bones and sinews).
Dissolve your whole body into Vision: become seeing, seeing, seeing!
One sight discerns but a yard or two of the road; another surveys the temporal and spiritual worlds and beholds the Face of their King.

VII. THE UNREGENERATE[1]

If any one were to say to the embryo in the womb, "Outside is a world well-ordered,
A pleasant earth, broad and long, wherein are a thousand delights and many things to eat;
Mountains and seas and plains, fragrant orchards, gardens and sown fields,
A sky very lofty and full of light, sunshine and moonbeams and innumerable stars;
Its wonders are beyond description: why dost thou stay, drinking blood, in this dungeon of filth and pain?"—
The embryo, being what it is, would turn away in utter disbelief; for the blind have no imagination.
So, in this world, when the saints tell of a world without scent and hue,
None of the vulgar hearkens to them: sensual desire is a barrier huge and stout—
Even as the embryo's craving for the blood that nourishes it in its low abodes
Debarred it from the perception of the external world, since it knows no food but blood.

---

[3]God is the only real Agent. All movement and life in the Universe proceeds from Him.

---

[1]*Math.* III, 53. The analogy of childbirth and weaning to spiritual regeneration is developed in many passages of the *Mathnawī*.

VIII.
THE BURDEN OF EXISTENCE[1]

From Thee first came this ebb and flow from within me; else, O Glorious One, my sea was still.
Now, from the same source whence Thou broughtest this trouble on me, graciously send me comfort!
O Thou Whose affliction makes men weak as women, show me the one path, do not let me follow ten!
I am like a jaded camel: the saddle of free-will has sorely bruised my back
With its heavy panniers sagging from this side to that in turn.
Let the ill-balanced load drop from me, so that I may browse in the Meadow of Thy Bounty.
Hundreds of thousands of years I was flying to and fro involuntarily, like a mote in the air.
If I have forgotten that time and state, yet the migration in sleep recalls it to my memory.
At night I escape from this four-branched cross into the spacious pastures of the spirit.[2]
From the nurse, Sleep, I suck the milk of those bygone days of mine, O Lord.
All mortals are fleeing from their free-will and self-existence to their unconscious selves.
They lay upon themselves the opprobrium of wine and minstrelsy in order that for awhile they may be delivered from self-consciousness.
All know that this existence is a snare, that will and thought and memory are a hell.

IX.
THE SPIRIT OF THE SAINTS[1]

There is a Water that flows down from Heaven
To cleanse the world of sin by grace Divine.
At last, its whole stock spent, its virtue gone,
Dark with pollution not its own, it speeds
Back to the Fountain of all purities;

[1]*Math.* VI, 210.
[2]See No. XIII. "This four-branched cross" alludes to the four elements which compose the prison-house where the fallen soul is crucified.

[1]*Math.* V, 200. Through absorption (*istighrāq*) in the Creator of spiritual energy the saints are revived and strengthened for their task "of pure ablution round earth's human shores."

Whence, freshly bathed, earthward it sweeps again,
Trailing a robe of glory bright and pure.

This Water is the Spirit of the Saints,
Which ever sheds, until itself is beggared,
God's balm on the sick soul; and then returns
To Him who made the purest light of Heaven.

X.
THE CHILDREN OF LIGHT[1]

Beyond the stars are Stars in which there is no combust nor sinister aspect,[2]
Stars moving in other Heavens, not the seven heavens known to all,
Stars immanent in the radiance of the Light of God, neither joined to each other nor separate.[3]
Whoso hath his fortune from these Stars, his soul drives off and consumes the unbelievers.[4]
God sprinkled His Light over all spirits, but only the blest held up their skirts to receive it;
And, having gained that largesse of light, they turned their faces away from all but God.[5]
That which is of the sea is going to the sea: it is going to the place whence it came—
From the mountain the swift-rushing torrent, and from our body the soul whose motion is inspired by love.[6]

---

[1]*Math.* I, 754.

[2]"Combust" (*iḥtirāq*), an astronomical term for the conjunction of one of the five planets (Venus, Mercury, Mars, Jupiter and Saturn) with the sun in the same degree of the Zodiac.

[3]While dispositions in the physical world are said to be influenced by the planets, the fortune of the elect comes from spiritual luminaries shining eternally in the heaven of the Divine Essence. These "Stars" are the Names and Attributes of God which determine every phase of the mystic's life. In so far as they are diverse in their effects they are not inseparable; but from a higher point of view they inhere in the Undifferentiated Essence and are identical with It and with each other.

[4]The radiant souls of the elect consume infidelity in the same way as shooting stars burn the devils pelted with them (*Qur'ān* LXVII, 5).

[5]According to the *Ḥadīth:* "God created the creatures in darkness, then He sprinkled some of His Light upon them. Those whom it reached took the right path, while those whom it missed went astray."

[6]Every "part" seeks its "whole": the "Fünkelein der Seele" is impelled by love towards the Universal Light whence it sprang.

XI.
LOVE, THE HIEROPHANT[1]

'Tis heart-ache lays the lover's passion bare:
No sickness with heart-sickness may compare.
Love is a malady apart, the sign
And astrolabe of mysteries Divine.[2]
Whether of heavenly mould or earthly cast,
Love still doth lead us Yonder at the last.[3]
Reason, explaining Love, can naught but flounder
Like ass in mire: Love is Love's own expounder.
Does not the sun himself the sun declare?[4]
Behold him! All the proof thou seek'st is there.

XII.
THE LOVE OF WOMAN[1]

If you rule your wife outwardly, yet inwardly you are ruled by her whom you desire,
This is characteristic of Man: in other animals love is lacking, and that shows their inferiority.[2]
The Prophet said that woman prevails over the wise, while ignorant men prevail over her; for in them the fierceness of the animal is immanent.
Love and tenderness are human qualities, anger and lust are animal qualities.

---

[1]*Math.* I, 109.

[2]"Man is God's astrolabe, and just as by means of an astrolabe the astronomer discovers the conditions of the celestial spheres and observes the motions and influences of the stars, so when Man has received from God the gift of self-knowledge, he continually beholds the manifestation of the Divine Beauty, which is without attributes and beyond description, by means of the astrolabe of his existence, which is a Divine mirror wherein that Beauty never ceases to be displayed." (*Fīhi mā fīhi*, 13).

[3]So Emerson: "Beholding in many souls the traits of the divine beauty, and separating in each soul that which is divine from the taint which it has contracted in the world, the lover ascends to the highest beauty, to the love and knowledge of the Divinity by steps on this ladder of created souls."

[4]*Āftāb āmad dalīl-i āftāb*, a famous and oft-repeated analogy.

---

[1]*Math.* I, 2431.

[2]Although animals relatively to Man are deficient in love, they "know what love is" and "he that is blind to love is inferior to a dog" (*Math.* V, 2008).

Woman is a ray of God: she is not the earthly beloved. She is creative: you might say she is not created.[3]

XIII.
DIVINE BEAUTY[1]

Kings lick the earth whereof the fair are made,
For God hath mingled in the dusty earth
A draught of Beauty from His choicest cup.
'Tis *that*, fond lover—not these lips of clay—
Thou art kissing with a hundred ecstasies,
Think, then, what must it be when undefiled!

XIV.
"I TURN TOWARD THEE"[1]

O Thou Who art my soul's comfort in the season of sorrow,
O Thou Who art my spirit's treasure in the bitterness of death!
That which the imagination hath not conceived, that which the understanding hath not seen,
Visiteth my soul from Thee; hence in worship I turn toward Thee.
By Thy Grace I keep fixed on eternity my amorous gaze,
Except, O King, the pomps that perish lead me astray.
The favour of him who brings glad tidings of Thee,
Even without Thy summons, is sweeter in mine ear than songs.
If the never-ceasing Bounty should offer kingdoms,
If the Hidden Treasure should set before me all that is,
I would bow down with my soul, I would lay my face in the dust,
I would cry, "Of all these the love of such an One for me!"

---

[3]Sweeping aside the veil of form, the poet beholds in woman the eternal Beauty, the inspirer and object of all love, and regards her, in her essential nature, as the medium through which that Beauty reveals itself and exercises creative activity. Ibnu'l-'Arabī went so far as to say that the most perfect vision of God is enjoyed by those who contemplate Him in woman.

---

[1]*Math.* V, 372.

---

[1]*Dīwān, SP*, VI.

XV.
THE TRUTH WITHIN US[1]

'Twas a fair orchard, full of trees and fruit
And vines and greenery. A Ṣūfī there
Sat with eyes closed, his head upon his knee,
Sunk deep in meditation mystical.
"Why," asked another, "dost thou not behold
These Signs of God the Merciful displayed
Around thee, which He bids us contemplate?"
"The signs," he answered, "I behold within;
Without is naught but symbols of the Signs."

What is all beauty in the world? The image,
Like quivering boughs reflected in a stream,
Of that eternal Orchard which abides
Unwithered in the hearts of Perfect Men.

XVI.
MYSTICS KNOW[1]

Since Wisdom is the true believer's stray camel,[2] he knows it with certainty, from whomsoever he may have heard of it,
And when he finds himself face to face with it, how should there be doubt? How can he mistake?
If you tell a thirsty man—"Here is a cup of water: drink!"—
Will he reply?—"This is mere assertion: let me alone, O liar, go away."
Or suppose a mother cries to her babe, "Come, I am mother: hark my child!"—
Will it say?—"Prove this to me, so that I may take comfort in thy milk."
When in the heart of a people there is spiritual perception, the face and voice of the prophet are as an evidentiary miracle.
When the prophet utters a cry from without, the soul of the people falls to worship within,

---

[1]*Math.* IV, 1358. An early parallel occurs in the legend of Rābi'ah al-'Adawiyyah. One day in spring-time she entered her house and bowed her head. "Come out," said the woman-servant, "and behold what God hath made." Rābi'ah answered, "Come in and behold the Maker."

---

[1]*Math.* II, 3591, a passage illustrating the Platonic doctrine of anamnesis and the self-evidence of truth revealed in mystical experience.
[2]A saying ascribed to 'Alī. The Faithful seek the knowledge of God which they possessed in past eternity and recognize it immediately when found.

Because never in the world will the soul's ear have heard a cry of the same kind as his.
That wondrous voice is heard by the soul in exile—the voice of God calling, "*Lo, I am nigh.*"[3]

XVII.
ASLEEP TO THE WORLD[1]

Every night Thou dost free our spirits from the body's snare and erase all impressions on the tablets (of memory).
Our spirits are set free every night from this cage, they are done with audience and talk and tale.
At night prisoners forget their prison, at night governors forget their power.
There is no sorrow, no thought of gain or loss, no idea of this person or that person.
Such is the state of the mystic, even when he is not asleep: God saith, "(*Thou wouldst deem them awake*) *whilst they slept.*"[2]
He is asleep, day and night, to the affairs of this world, like a pen in the hand of the Lord.[3]
God hath shown forth some part of his state, inasmuch as the vulgar too are carried away by sleep:
Their spirits gone into the Wilderness that is beyond words, Their souls and bodies at rest.
Till with a whistle Thou callest them back to the snare, bringest them all again to justice and judgement.[4]
At daybreak, like Isrāfīl (Seraphiel), He bids them return from Yonder to the world of form:[5]
The disembodied spirits He confines anew and causes each body to be laden (with its good and evil works).

---

[3]*Qur'ān* II, 182.

---

[1]*Math.* I, 388.

[2]An allusion to the legend of the Seven Sleepers of Ephesus related in *Qur'ān* XVIII, 8–25.

[3]Cf. the Tradition that "the true believer is between the two fingers of God the Merciful." According as God reveals Himself in the aspect of Majesty (wrath and terror) or Beauty (mercy and love) the mystic's heart contracts with grief or expands with joy.

[4]*i.e.* to their self-conscious life in the present world, which is a court of Divine justice where mankind are on trial.

[5]This action of God resembles that of the Archangel Isrāfīl, whose trumpet-blast at the Resurrection will give the signal for the spirits of the dead to rejoin their bodies.

XVIII.
THE FAITHFUL ARE ONE SOUL[1]

The Faithful are many, but their Faith is one; their bodies are numerous, but their soul is one.

Besides the understanding and soul which is in the ox and the ass, Man has another intelligence and soul.

Again, in the owner of the Divine breath, there is a soul other than the human soul.[2]

The animal soul does not possess oneness: do not seek oneness from that airy spirit.

If its owner eat bread, his neighbour is not filled; if he bear a load, his neighbour does not become laden;

Nay, but he rejoices at his neighbour's death and dies of envy when he sees his neighbour prosperous.

The souls of wolves and dogs are separate; the souls of the Lions of God are united.

I speak nominally of their souls in the plural, for that single Soul is a hundred in relation to the body,

Just as the single light of the sun in heaven is a hundred in relation to the house-courts on which it shines;

But when you remove the walls, all these scattered lights are one and the same.

When the bodily houses have no foundation remaining, the Faithful remain one soul.

XIX.
THE LADDER TO HEAVEN[1]

The worldly sense is the ladder to this world; the religious sense is the ladder to Heaven.

Seek the well-being of that sense from the physician; beg the well-being of this sense from the man beloved of God.[2]

The spiritual way ruins the body and, having ruined it, restores it to prosperity:

---

[1]*Math.* IV, 408. When Rūmī speaks of "the Faithful," he generally means inspired men, who alone have the real faith that springs from immediate experience of the Divine.

[2]The three souls mentioned here are known in Ṣūfī psychology as (*a*) the animal or sensual; (*b*) the intelligential (discursive reason); and (*c*) the transcendental (Universal Reason), which displays itself in prophets and saints.

---

[1]*Math.* I, 303.

[2]*i.e.* the saintly healer of souls.

Ruined the house for the sake of the golden treasure, and with that same treasure builds it better than before;[3]
Cut off the water and cleansed the river-bed, then caused drinking-water to flow in it;[4]
Cleft the skin and drew out the barb, then made fresh skin grow over the wound;
Razed the fortress and took it from the infidel, then reared thereon a hundred towers and ramparts.[5]
Sometimes the action of God appears like this, sometimes the contrary: (true) religion is nothing but bewilderment.
(I mean) not one bewildered in such wise that his back is turned on Him; nay, but one bewildered and drowned and drunken with the Beloved.[6]
His face is set towards (devoted to) the Beloved, while the other's face is just his own.
Look long on the face of everyone, watch attentively: it may be that by doing service (to Ṣūfīs) you will come to know the face (of the Saint).
Since many a devil hath the face of Adam, you should not put a hand in every hand;
For as the fowler whistles to decoy a bird he is bent on catching,
Which hears the note of its mate and comes down from the air and finds itself entrapped,
So does a vile man steal the language of dervishes to fascinate and deceive one who is simple.
The work of holy men is as light and heat; the work of the ungodly is trickery and shamelessness.

---

[3]The spiritual essence of Man is buried in his earthly nature, as a treasure beneath the floor of a house.

[4]Purification of the heart cannot begin till the "water" of lust, passion, and all sensuous ideas has been cut off.

[5]Ghazālī likens the body to a fortress in which God has placed the spirit or rational soul with orders to defend it against the "infidel," *i.e.* the carnal soul. When it is occupied by evil passions, the spirit must destroy it, expel the invaders, and then rebuild it and make it impregnable.

[6]The discursive reason, contemplating apparently irreconcilable forms of Divine action, is bewildered. But the bewilderment (*ḥayrat*) of mystics dazzled by nearness to the Light of God must not be confused with that of religious hypocrites who have lost their way in a maze of ignorance and error.

XX.
THE TRUE ṢŪFĪ[1]

What makes the Ṣūfī? Purity of heart;
Not the patched mantle and the lust perverse
Of those vile earth-bound men who steal his name.
He in all dregs discerns the essence pure:
In hardship ease, in tribulation joy.
The phantom sentries, who with batons drawn
Guard Beauty's palace-gate and curtained bower,
Give way before him, unafraid he passes,
And showing the King's arrow, enters in.[2]

XXI.
NOTHING VENTURE NOTHING WIN[1]

When you put a cargo on board a ship, you make that venture on trust,
For you know not whether you will be drowned or come safe to land.
If you say, "I will not embark till I am certain of my fate," then you will do no trade: the secret of these two destinies is never disclosed.
The faint-hearted merchant neither gains nor loses; nay he loses: one must take fire in order to get light.
Since all affairs turn upon hope, surely Faith is the best object of hope, for thereby you win salvation.

---

[1]*Math.* V, 358.

[2]An arrow inscribed with the king's name was handed to a surrendering enemy in token that his safety was guaranteed. Sa'dī alludes to this custom in the verse:
"Either thou wilt shoot a deadly arrow at my wounded heart
And take my life, or thou wilt give me the arrow of indemnity (*tīr-i amān*)."

---

[1]*Math.* III, 3083. Though God has decreed in eternity that some souls are saved and others lost, He commands the prophets to preach His Word to all alike (*Qur'ān* V, 71). Obey it and trust in Him. Even worldly success cannot be achieved without running risks.

XXII.
THE MAN WHO LOOKED BACK ON HIS WAY TO HELL[1]

The guardian angels, who used to walk unseen before and behind him, have now become visible like policemen.
They drag him along, prodding him with goads and crying, "Begone, O dog, to thy kennel!"
He looks back towards the Holy Presence: his tears fall like autumn rain. A mere hope—what has he but that?
Then from God in the realm of Light comes the command— "Say ye to him: 'O ne'er-do-well destitute of merit,
Thou hast seen the black scroll of thy misdeeds. What dost thou expect? Why art thou tarrying in vain?'"
He answers: "Lord, Thou knowest I am a hundred hundred times worse than Thou hast declared;
But beyond my exertion and action, beyond good and evil and faith and infidelity,
Beyond living righteously or behaving disobediently—I had a great hope of Thy Loving-kindness.
I turn again to that pure Grace, I am not regarding my own works.
Thou gavest me my being as a robe of honour: I have always relied on that munificence."
When he confesses his sins, God saith to the Angels, "Bring him back, for he never lost hope of Me.
Like one who recks of naught, I will deliver him and cancel all his trespasses.
I will kindle such a fire of Grace that the least spark thereof consumes all sin and necessity and free-will.
I will set fire to the tenement of Man and make its thorns a bower of roses."

---

[1]*Math.* V, 1815. The passage to which these verses belong is founded on the following tradition: "When God has finished judging mankind on the Day of Resurrection, two men will remain and the order will be given that both are for Hell. Then on the way thither one of them will turn his face to God, and the Almighty will order him to be brought back and will ask him why he turned round, and he will answer, 'I was hoping Thou wouldst let me enter Paradise.' And then God will order that he be taken to Paradise."

XXIII.
SPIRITUAL CHURNING[1]

Thy truth is concealed in falsehood, like the taste of butter in buttermilk.
Thy falsehood is this perishable body; thy truth is the lordly spirit.
During many years the buttermilk remains in view, while the butter has vanished as though it were naught,
Till God send a Messenger, a chosen Servant, to shake the buttermilk in the churn—
To shake it with method and skill, and teach me that my true self was hidden.[2]
The buttermilk is old: keep it, do not let it go till you extract the butter from it.
Turn it deftly to and fro, that it may give up its secret.
The mortal body is a proof of the immortal spirit: the maundering of the drunken reveller proves the existence of the cupbearer.

XXIV.
THE BLIND FOLLOWER[1]

The parrot looking in the mirror sees
Itself, but not its teacher hid behind,
And learns the speech of Man, the while it thinks
A bird of its own sort is talking to it.[2]

So the disciple full of egoism
Sees nothing in the Shaykh except himself.
The Universal Reason eloquent
Behind the mirror of the Shaykh's discourse—
The Spirit which is the mystery of Man—
He cannot see. Words mimicked, learned by rote,
'Tis all. A parrot he, no bosom-friend!

---

[1] *Math.* IV, 3030.

[2] It is the mission of the Sūfī Pīr to develop and bring out the spiritual qualities latent in his disciple, just as an infant learns to speak by listening to its mother.

---

[1] *Math.* V, 1430.

[2] Parrots in the East are trained to talk by means of a mirror, behind which is a curtain. Allegorically the "mirror" is the holy man, who serves as a medium between the "parrot," *i.e.* the disciple, and God, the invisible Speaker and Teacher.

XXV. THE BIRDS OF SOLOMON[1]

The eloquence of courtly birds is a mere echo: where is the speech of the birds of Solomon?[2]
How wilt thou know their cries, when thou hast never seen Solomon for a single moment?
Far beyond East and West are spread the wings of the bird whose note thrills them that hear it:
From the Footstool of God to the earth and from the earth to the Divine Throne it moves in glory and majesty.
The bird that goes without this Solomon is a bat in love with darkness.
Make thyself familiar with Solomon, O miscreant bat, lest thou remain in darkness for ever.
Go but one ell in that direction, and like the ell thou wilt become the standard of measurement.[3]
Even by hopping lamely and limply in that direction thou wilt be freed from all lameness and limpness.

XXVI. THE CARNAL SOUL[1]

Your self (*nafs*) is the mother of all idols: the material idol is a snake, but the spiritual idol is a dragon.
'Tis easy to break an idol, very easy; to regard the self as easy to subdue is folly, folly.
O son, if you would know the form of the self, read the description of Hell with its seven gates.[2]
From the self at every moment issues an act of deceit; and in each of those deceits a hundred Pharaohs and their hosts are drowned.

---

[1]*Math.* II, 3758. Solomon was taught the bird language (*Qur'ān* XXVII, 16). Here he represents the Perfect Man, *i.e.* the Sūfī *murshid.*

[2]All artificial eloquence, such as court poets display in their panegyrics, is meaningless in comparison with the mystic utterances of those whom God has inspired.

[3]Cf. the saying of Kharraqānī, "I attained to God as soon as I set foot on the first step of the ladder." The Perfect Man is the ideal of creation and the criterion by which the true value of everything is to be judged.

---

[1]*Math.* I, 772.

[2]The *nafs* is Hell or a part of Hell; in essence it is one with the Devil. Therefore Hell, being the nature of the *nafs-i ammārah* (the soul that commands us to sin), is really subjective. The seven gates or limbos of Hell typify the vices which lead to perdition (*muhlikāt*).

XXVII.
THE BEAUTY OF DEATH[1]

He who deems to be lovely as Joseph gives up his soul in ransom for it; he who deems it to be like the wolf turns back from the path of salvation.

Every one's death is of the same quality as himself, my lad: to the enemy of God an enemy, to the friend of God a friend.[2]

In the eyes of the Turcoman the mirror is fair; in the eyes of the Ethiopian it is dark as an Ethiopian.

Your fear of death is really fear of yourself: see what it is from which you are fleeing!

'Tis your own ugly face, not the visage of Death: your spirit is like the tree, and death like the leaf.

It has grown from you, whether it be good or evil: all your hidden thoughts, foul or fair, are born from yourself.

If you are wounded by thorns, you planted them; and if you are clad in satin and silk, *you* were the spinner.

Know that the act is not of the same complexion as its result; a service rendered is not homogeneous with the fragment given in return.

The labourer's wage is dissimilar to his work: the latter is the accident, while the former is the substance.[3]

The latter is wholly toil and effort and sweat, the former is wholly silver and gold and viands.

When the worshipper has sown a prostration or genuflexion here, it becomes the Garden of the Blest hereafter.

When praise of God has flown from his mouth, the Lord of the Daybreak fashions it into a fruit of Paradise.

---

[1]*Math.* III, 3438. Cf. No. VI. The comparison with Joseph and the wolf alludes to *Qur'ān* XII, 13 *seqq.*

[2]Death, whether physical (*iḍṭirārī*) or mystical (*ikhtiyārī*), is like a mirror in which every one sees the image of himself: if his nature be good and his actions righteous, he will be in love with death; otherwise he will loathe it and flee in terror from the reflection of his own wickedness. What he dreads so much is really something conceived and produced by himself.

[3]Human action is both a cause and an effect. Man, in so far as he acts freely, incurs retribution hereafter; but this, though from one point of view a direct consequence of the action with which it corresponds in quality, may also be regarded as the final cause and eternal form of the action, pre-existent in God's Knowledge, like the idea of a house in the mind of the architect. Viewed in this way, retribution is a Divine manifestation of the idea immanent in all that appears under the form of human action or, in other words, a transformation of the appearance with its underlying reality. Hence there can be no true similarity between them: they differ as accident and substance. See further, *Math.* II, 938–1000 with the commentary *ad loc.*

XXVIII.
A PRAYER FOR GOOD BEHAVIOUR[1]

Let us beseech God to help us to self-control (*adab*): he who lacks self-control is deprived of the grace of the Lord.[2]
The undisciplined man does not corrupt himself alone: he sets the whole world afire.
Whatever befalls thee of gloom and sorrow is the result of thy irreverence and insolence.
Any one behaving with irreverence in the path of the Friend is a brigand who robs men: he is no man.[3]
Through discipline Heaven was filled with light, through discipline the Angels became immaculate and holy.[4]
By reason of irreverence the sun is eclipsed, and insolence caused 'Azāzīl to be turned back from the door.[5]

XXIX.
COMMUNION WITH THE SAINTS[1]

God rebuked Moses, saying. "O thou who hast seen the rising of the moon from thy bosom,[2]
Thou whom I have illumined with My Light! I am God, I fell sick, thou camest not."[3]
Moses said, "O transcendent One, Thou art clear of defect. What mystery is this? Explain, O Lord!"
God said unto him again, "Wherefore didst not thou kindly ask after Me when I was sick?"

---

[1]*Math.* I, 78.
[2]*Adab* may be defined as the character, feelings, and manners which are the fruit of self-discipline and spiritual culture; like St. Paul's ἀγάπη "it doth not behave itself unseemly."
[3]He has not mastered his passions and therefore does not deserve the name of "man."
[4]Cf. Wordsworth's lines in the *Ode to Duty:*
"Thou dost preserve the Stars from wrong,
And the most ancient Heavens, through thee, are fresh and strong."
[5]Eclipse is a Divine chastisement inflicted on the sun whenever it presumed to deviate from its appointed course. 'Azāzīl was the name of Iblīs before his fall.

---

[1]*Math.* II, 2156.
[2]Mystic illumination is often likened to the White Hand of Moses. See *Qur'ān* VII, 105 and Exodus IV, 6.
[3]This passage on the oneness of God with His friends (*awliyā*) gives the gist of a Holy Tradition (*Ḥadīth-i qudsī*), beginning: "On the Day of Resurrection God most High will say, 'O Son of Adam, I was sick and thou didst not visit Me.'" Cf. St. Matthew, XXV, 43–45.

He answered. "O Lord, Thou never ailest. My understanding is lost: unfold the meaning of these words."
God said. "Yea; a favourite and chosen slave of Mine fell sick. I am he. Consider well:
His infirmity is My infirmity, his sickness is My sickness."
Who ever would sit with God, let him sit in the presence of the Saints.
If you are separated from the presence of the Saints, you are in perdition, because you are a part without its whole.
Whomsoever the Devil cuts off from that noble company, he finds him with none to aid and devours him.

XXX.
THE MAN WHO FLED FROM AZRAEL[1]

At morn, to Solomon in his hall of justice
A noble suitor came, running in haste,
His countenance pale with anguish, his lips blue.
"What ails, thee, Khwājah?" asked the King.
Then he:
"'Twas Azrael—ah, such a look he cast
On me of rage and vengeance." "Come now, ask
What boon thou wilt." "Protector of our lives,
I pray theè, bid the Wind convey me straight
To Hindustān: thy servant, there arrived,
Shall peradventure save his soul from Death."

How folk do ever flee from dervishhood
Into the jaws of greed and idle hope!
Your fear of dervishhood is that doomed man's terror,
Greed and ambition are your Hindustān.[2]
Solomon bade the Wind transport him swiftly
Over the sea to farthest Hindustān.
On the morrow, when the King in audience sate,
He said to Azrael, "Wherefore didst thou look
Upon that Musulmān so wrathfully
His home knew him no more?" "Nay, not in wrath,"
Replied the Angel, "did I look on him;
But seeing him pass by, I stared in wonder,

---

[1]*Math.* I, 956.
[2]"Dervishhood" is spiritual poverty, which means "dying to self," *i.e.* abandoning every "god" or object of desire except Allah. To shrink from this "death" and seek satisfaction in the pursuit of worldly goods is as vain and useless as to flee from Azrael.

For God had bidden me take his soul that day
In Hindustān. I stood there marvelling.
Methought, even if he had a hundred wings,
'Twere far for him to fly to Hindustān."

Judge all things of the world by this same rule
And ope your eyes and see! Away from whom
Shall we fly headlong? From ourselves?
  Absurd!
From God, then? Oh, the vain and woeful crime![3]

XXXI.
"OMNES EODEM COGIMUR"[1]

Every blind wayfarer, be he righteous or wicked, God is dragging, bound in chains, into His Presence.
All are dragged along this Way reluctantly, save those who are acquainted with the mysteries of Divine action.
The command *Come against your will* is addressed to the blind follower; *Come willingly* is for the man moulded of truth.[2]
While the former, like an infant, loves the Nurse for the sake of milk, the other has given his heart away to this Veiled One.
The "infant" hath no knowledge of Her beauty: he wants nothing of Her except milk;
The real lover of the Nurse is disinterested, single-minded in pure devotion.
Whether God's seeker love Him for something other than He, that he may continually partake of His good,
Or whether he love God for His Very Self, for naught besides Him, lest he be separated from Him,
In either case the quest and aspiration proceed from that Source: the heart is made captive by that Heart-ravisher.

---

[3]It is absurd to suppose that we can escape from being what God has predetermined and created us to be. Our freedom consists in not being slaves to our passions or to anything whatsoever but God alone.

---

[1]*Math.* III, 4581.
[2]See *Qur'ān* XLI, 10 and No. XCII *infra.*

XXXII.
FAITH AND WORKS[1]

God hath placed a ladder before us: we must climb it, step by step.
You have feet: why pretend to be lame? You have hands: why conceal the fingers that grip?
Freewill is the endeavour to thank God for His Beneficence; your necessitarianism denies that Beneficence.
Thanksgiving for the power of acting freely gives you more power to thank Him; necessitarianism takes away what God hath given.
The brigands are on the road: do not sleep until you see the gate and the threshold![2]
If you put trust in God, trust Him with your work! Sow the seed, then rely upon the Almighty![3]

XXXIII.
"NO MONKERY IN ISLAM"[1]

"O peacock, do not tear out thy feathers, but wean thy heart from pride in them: the existence of a foe is indispensable for waging the Holy War.
There cannot be self-restraint in the absence of desire: when there is no adversary, what avails thy courage?
Hark, do not castrate thyself, do not become a monk: chastity depends on the existence of lust.

---

[1]*Math.* I, 929. The arguments for and against quietism (*tawakkul*, trust in God) are set forth in the form of a dialogue between a lion and the smaller animals on which he preys (*Math.* I, 900–991). *Tawakkul*, no doubt, is fundamental; but does it imply that we should refrain from using to the best of our ability the faculties of mind and body which God has bestowed on us in order that we may attain to real Knowledge of Him? On the contrary, to neglect these means (*asbāb*) is rank impiety and ingratitude. Our throwing ourselves earnestly into the spiritual warfare (*al-jihād al-akbar*), far from being a vain attempt to interfere with the course of Providence, is a Divinely ordained duty, which all prophets and saints have practised as well as preached.

[2]The "traveller" (*sālik*) on the Way to God must never rest. Only when the goal is gained can he afford to "sleep," *i.e.* enjoy the mystical state of quiet.

[3]Cf. the Prophet's advice to one who asked whether he should leave his camel to God's care: "Tether her, then trust in Him."

---

[1]*Math.* V, 574. This apocryphal Ḥadīth, based on a questionable interpretation of a passage in the *Qur'ān* (LVII, 27), is aimed at asceticism as practised by Christian hermits; and here Rūmī contrasts the Ṣūfī Path of self-discipline and self-conquest with a method which, in cutting off all temptations, deprives itself of the means whereby virtue is tested and wisdom made perfect.

The Divine command *'Eat ye'* is the lure for appetite; then comes *'Do not exceed'*: that is temperance.[2]
Without the pain of self-denial there is no protasis; hence the apodosis does not follow.[3]
How admirable is that protasis and how delightful is that apodosis—a recompense enchanting the heart and increasing the life of the spirit!"

XXXIV.
DO NOT TRAVEL ALONE[1]

In our religion the approved thing is war and danger; in the religion of Jesus it is flight to cave and mountain.[2]
The Sunnah is the safest road, and the community of the Faithful your best fellow-travellers.
The Way to God is full of trouble and bale: it is not the way for any one whose nature is effeminate.
On this road men's souls are tried by terror, as a sieve is used for sifting bran.
If you go by yourself, I grant that you may manage to escape the wolf; but you will feel no spiritual alacrity.
The ass, notwithstanding its grossness, is encouraged and strengthened, O dervish, by comrades of its own kind.
How many more goadings and cudgellings does it suffer when it crosses the desert without company!
It says to you implicitly, "Take good heed! Don't travel alone unless you are an ass!"

---

[2]See *Qur'ān* VII, 29.
[3]A grammatical analogy. The Ṣūfī's reward from God depends on his self-denial in the same way as the consequence stated in the principal clause of a conditional sentence depends on fulfilment of the condition stated in the subordinate clause.

---

[1]*Math.* VI, 494.
[2]Rūmī adopts the traditional Moslem view of "the religion of Jesus," a view derived from early Moslem ascetics who took the solitary *rāhib* as their model, while Ṣūfīs, with few exceptions, have not only embraced but developed the idea of brotherhood so characteristic of religious life in Islam.

XXXV.
FINE FEATHERS[1]

"Needs must I tear them out," the peacock cried,
"These gorgeous plumes which only tempt my pride."

Of all his talents let the fool beware:
Mad for the bait, he never sees the snare.
Harness to fear of God thy strength and skill,
Else there's no bane so deadly as free-will.

XXXVI.
THE TREASURE-SEEKER[1]

He was engaged in this prayer when a Voice came from Heaven, saying,
"You were told to put the arrow to the bow; but who told you to shoot with all your might?
Self-conceit caused you to raise the bow aloft and display your skill in archery.
You must put the arrow to the bow, but do not draw to the full extent of your power.
Where the arrow falls, dig and search! Trust not in strength, seek the treasure by means of piteous supplication."

That which is real is nearer than the neck-artery, and you have shot the arrow of thought far afield.[2]
The philosopher kills himself with thinking. Let him run on: his back is turned to the treasure.

---

[1]*Math.* V, 648. Human powers and capacities, unless devoted to the service of God, breed false confidence and bring disaster. The moral, however, is not that we must deliberately throw away the weapons without which the victory over ourselves cannot be won, but that we should beware of relying on them and taking credit for any success they enable us to achieve.

---

[1]*Math.* VI, 2347. A dervish dreamed that a Voice from Heaven bade him go to the shop of a certain stationer, where he would find a scroll containing the clue to a hidden treasure. On awaking, he went to the shop and, having found the scroll, read it with care, followed the directions exactly, and persevered in the quest for a long time, but all his efforts were unavailing till he gave up hope and besought God to help him.
[2]"Nearer than the neck-artery." See *Qur'ān* L, 15.

Most of those destined for Paradise are simpletons, so that they escape from the mischief of philosophy.[3]

While the clever ones are pleased with the device, the simple ones rest, like babes, in the bosom of the Deviser.

XXXVII.

THE MYSTIC WAY[1]

Plug thy low sensual ear, which stuffs like cotton
Thy conscience and makes deaf thine inward ear.
Be without ear, without sense, without thought,
And hearken to the call of God, "*Return!*"
Our speech and action is the outer journey,
Our inner journey is above the sky[2]
The body travels on its dusty way;
The spirit walks, like Jesus, on the sea.

XXXVIII.

THE SCEPTIC[1]

The philosopher who disbelieves in the Moaning Pillar is a stranger to the senses of the saints.[2]

He says the influence of melancholia brings many phantasies into people's minds.

Nay, this idle fancy of his is but the reflexion of his own wickedness and infidelity.

He denies the existence of the Devil, and at the same time he is possessed by a devil.

If thou hast not seen the Devil, behold thyself! Without diabolic possession there is no blueness in the forehead.

---

[3]For the meaning of simpleton (*ablah*) in this well-known Ḥadīth, cf. Epistle to the Romans, XV, 19: "wise unto that which is good and simple unto that which is evil." "Their foolishness," says Sulṭān Walad, "is the highest wisdom: knowing nought of any but the Beloved, of Him they are extremely conscious and aware."

---

[1]*Math.* I, 566.
[2]The *introrsum ascendere* of medieval Christian mysticism.

---

[1]*Math.* I, 3280.
[2]The miracle of the pillar (a palm-trunk in the Prophet's mosque at Medina), against which he used to lean while preaching, is related in *Math.* I, 2113 *seqq.* Subsequently a pulpit was set up for him, and when he seated himself the deserted pillar "moaned and cried till it was well-nigh split."

Whosoever feels doubt in his heart is a secret philosopher.
He may profess firm belief, but some time or other that philosophical vein will blacken his face for all to see.
Take care, O ye Faithful! That vein is in you: within you is many an infinite world.[3]
Within you are all the two-and-seventy sects: woe to you if one day they put forth their heads![4]

XXXIX.
THE EVIL IN OURSELVES[1]

The Lion took the Hare with him: they ran together to the well and looked in.
The Lion saw his own image: from the water appeared the form of a lion with a plump hare beside him.
No sooner did he espy his enemy than he left the Hare and sprang into the well.
He fell into the pit which he had dug: his iniquity recoiled on his own head.

O Reader, how many an evil that you see in others is but your own nature reflected in them!
In them appears all that *you* are—your hypocrisy, iniquity, and insolence.
You do not see clearly the evil in yourself, else you would hate yourself with all your soul.
Like the Lion who sprang at his image in the water, you are only hurting yourself, O foolish man.
When you reach the bottom of the well of your own nature, then you will know that the wickedness is in *you*.

---

[3]*i.e.* conceptions and imaginations without end.
[4]The Prophet is said to have predicted that the Moslem community would be divided into seventy-three sects, of which only one would enter Paradise, the remainder being destined for Hell-fire.

---

[1]*Math.* I, 1306. In Rūmī's version of this Indian fable, the carnal self (*nafs*) is represented as the lion who was lured by a hare to the mouth of a deep well where, mistaking his own reflexion for a hated rival, he sprang in and perished miserably. For the doctrine that all so-called evil is an illusion arising from the diversity of Divine Attributes—Beauty and Majesty, Mercy and Wrath, etc.—reflected in human nature, and that only our egoism prevents us from seeing the "soul of goodness" everywhere, cf. Nos. LXXXIX–XCV *infra.* So far as evil exists in us, its source is the unreal "self" (*nafs*) by which we are separated from God. Purge the heart of "self," and evil disappears.

XL.
THE HIERARCHY OF SAINTS[1]

In every epoch after Mohammed a Saint arises to act as his viceregent: the people are on trial till the Resurrection.[2]
Whosoever has a good nature is saved, whosoever is of frail heart is broken.
The Saint, then, is the living Imām, who appears in every age, whether he be a descendant of 'Umar or of 'Alī.[3]
He is the God-guided one (Mahdī) and the Guide (Hādī): he is both hidden and seated before you.[4]
He is as the Light of the Prophet, and Universal Reason is his Gabriel: the saint lesser than he receives illumination from him, like a lamp.[5]
The saint below this "lamp" is as the lamp-niche: the Light has gradations of intensity;[6]
For the Light of God has seven hundred veils: regard the veils of the Light as so many tiers.[7]
Behind each veil a certain class of saints has its abode: the veils mount tier after tier up to the Imām.

---

[1]*Math.* II, 815.

[2]The saying attributed to Mohammed, "there shall be no prophet after me," was supplemented by Traditions concerning his spiritual heirs and successors—a hierarchy ranged in classes of gradually increasing size under the supreme saint (*Quṭb*) of the age—who act as touchstones whereby truth and falsehood are discriminated. So long as the world endures, this process of testing (*āzmāyish*) will go on, and whatever the hypocrite may profess, his attitude towards the Saints will always betray his real character.

[3]Here the poet draws a sharp line between the Twelve Shī'ite Imāms, descended from 'Alī (of whom the last vanished mysteriously but is expected to reappear as the Mahdī at the end of the world) and the uninterrupted succession of great Ṣūfī saints, who have no common ancestry except their purely spiritual descent from the Prophet in virtue of the "Light of Mohammed" (*Nūr-i Muḥammadī*) immanent in them all.

[4]The *Quṭb* is a "Mahdī" and a "Hidden Imām," but only in the sense that he is the Divinely-guided Perfect Man who makes others perfect (*Kāmil ū mukmil*), and that although seen by many he is recognized by few.

[5]Having realized his essential unity with God, he transcends even Universal Reason, the first individualization of the Absolute, just as Mohammed in his Ascension left Gabriel behind at the moment when he was about to enter the Divine presence (*Qur'ān* LIII). Probably the "lamp" denotes one of the exalted saints known as *Abdāl* or *Awtād*.

[6]"The lamp-niche" (*mishkāt*) alludes to a celebrated verse of the *Qur'ān* (XXIV, 35): "Allah is the Light of the heavens and the earth; the likeness of His Light is a niche wherein is a lamp."

[7]The Ḥadīth concerning seven hundred (or seventy thousand) veils of light and darkness which conceal the Face of Allah is expounded by Ghazālī in his *Mishkāt al-Anwār*. See Gairdner's translation, 88–98. The light-veils correspond to various degrees of saintship.

The light that is the life of the topmost rank is painful and insupportable to one beneath;
Yet, by degrees, his squintness diminishes; and when he has passed through all seven hundred veils, he becomes the Sea.[8]
The fire that is good for iron or gold—how should it be good for quinces and apples?
The apple and quince have only a slight crudity: unlike iron, they want a gentle heat;
But those flames are too mild for the iron, which easily absorbs the glow of the fiery dragon.
What is that iron? The self-mortified dervish: under the hammer and the fire he is red and happy.
He is the chamberlain of the fire, in immediate touch with it: he goes straight into the heart of the fire.
Therefore he is the Heart of the world, for by means of the heart the body performs its proper function.
All individual hearts are as the body in relation to the universal Heart of the Saint.

XLI.
THE SPIRITUAL GUIDE[1]

The Prophet said to 'Alī: "O 'Alī, thou art the Lion of God, thou art a valiant knight,
But do not rely upon thy courage: come into the shadow of the Palm-tree of hope.
Come into the shadow (protection) of the Sage whom none can waylay.
His shadow on the earth is like Mt. Qāf, his spirit is like the Sīmurgh that soars aloft.[2]

---

[8]"He becomes the Sea," *i.e.* he is completely submerged in the Essence. The following verses illustrate the inequality of spiritual capacity and endowment. The weaker brethren cannot dispense with the mediation of a Perfect Man inured to the fire of Divine Love, by which they themselves, if brought into direct contact with it, would be utterly destroyed before they were "cooked."

---

[1]*Math.* I, 2959. One of many passages in which the poet emphasizes the need of saintly help and guidance for those who would take up arms in "the greater Holy War" (*al-jihād al-akbar*) against the flesh, the world, and the Devil.
[2]Qāf, the inaccessible mountain-range that is supposed to engirdle the (flat) earth and said to be the home of the Sīmurgh, a mythical bird which in Ṣūfism represents God or the soul regarded as a mode of Divine Being.

Though I should sing his praises until the Resurrection, do not look for any end to them.
The Divine Sun has veiled Himself in Man: apprehend this mystery, and God knows best what is the truth.
O 'Alī, above all works of devotion in the Way is the shadow of God's Servant.[3]
When others seek to save themselves by religious works,
Go thou, take refuge in the shadow of the Sage against the enemy within thee."
Having been accepted by the Pīr, give thyself up to him: submit, like Moses, to the authority of Khizr.[4]
Whatever the Khizr may do, bear it patiently, lest he say, "Begone, *here we part.*"
Though he scuttle the boat, be dumb! Though he kill a child, do not tear thy hair!
God hath described his hand as His own, for He saith, "*The Hand of God is over their hands.*"[5]
This "Hand of God" slays his disciple, then brings him to life everlasting.[6]

XLII.
THE USES OF TRIBULATION[1]

Look at a chickpea in the pot, how it leaps up when it is subjected to the fire.
Whilst it is boiling, it always comes up to the top, crying ceaselessly,
"Why are you setting the fire on me? You bought me: why are you tormenting me like this?"
The housewife goes on hitting it with the ladle. "Now," says she, "boil nicely and don't jump away from her who makes the fire.

[3]The Perfect Man, notwithstanding his virtual "deification," is pre-eminently "God's Servant" (*'abdu 'llāh*), a title given to Mohammed (*Qur'ān* LXXII, 19). He serves none other than God and has lost himself in the Object of his devotion.
[4]The unquestioning obedience which every Ṣūfī Shaykh demands from his disciples is often illustrated by reference to the well-known story of Khizr (Khaḍir) and Moses in *Qur'ān* XVIII, 64 *seqq*. Holy men can justify all their actions, however incomprehensible and seemingly immoral these may be.
[5]*Qur'ān* XLVIII, 10: "Verily, those who swear fealty to thee (the Prophet) swear fealty to Allah: the Hand of Allah is over their hands."
[6]The *murshid*, acting as God's instrument, causes the disciple (*murīd*) to die to self (*fanā*) and live in God (*baqā*).

[1]*Math.* III, 4159. The "housewife" is the *murshid*, the "chickpea" the *murīd*, and the "fire" the Ṣūfī discipline of self-mortification.

I boil thee, but not because thou art hateful to me; nay, 'tis that thou mayst get savour
And become nutriment and mingle with the vital spirit: such affliction is no abasement.
When thou wert green and fresh, thou drankest water in the garden: that water-drinking was for the sake of this fire.
God's mercy is prior to His wrath, to the end that by His mercy thou mayst suffer tribulation.[2]
His mercy preceded His wrath in order that the stock-in-trade, which is existence, should be produced;
For without pleasure flesh and skin do not grow, and unless they grow, what shall Divine Love consume?
If, because of that requirement, acts of wrath come to pass to the end that thou shouldst give up thy stock-in-trade,
Yet afterwards the Grace of God will justify them, saying 'Now thou art washed clean and hast jumped out of the river.'
Continue, O chickpea, to boil in tribulation until neither existence nor self remains to thee.
If thou hast been severed from the garden of earth, yet thou wilt be food in the mouth and enter into the living.[3]
Be nutriment, energy, thought! Thou wert milky sap: now be a lion of the jungle!
Thou grewest from God's Attributes in the beginning: pass again into His Attributes!
Thou wert a part of the cloud and the sun and the stars: thou wilt become soul and action and speech and thought.
The life of the animal arose from the death of the plant: hence the injunction, 'Slay me, O trusty friends,' is right.
Since such a victory awaits us after death, the words, 'Lo, in being slain I live,' are true."[4]

---

[2]There are Traditions in which God declares that His mercy precedes or prevails over His wrath. Divine Love brought us into existence, and its object cannot be realized without purging and transmuting our fleshly qualities (*ṣifātu 'l-bashariyyah*).

[3]In this and the following verses, spiritual evolution (see No. CXVIII *infra*) is symbolized by the process through which a chickpea, when cooked, eaten, assimilated, and converted into sperm, loses its vegetable nature, participates in the animal life of man, ascends to rationality, and eventually returns to the world of Divine Attributes from which it came.

[4]The words "slay me, O trusty friends" and "in being slain I live" are quoted from an Arabic ode by Ḥallāj, the most famous of Ṣūfī martyrs.

XLIII.
"THE SPIRIT HELPETH OUR INFIRMITY"[1]

The good thou art set upon, whate'er it be,
Its imperfection hath been hid from thee;
For were the vice laid bare, thy loathing soul
Would turn and fly from pole to farthest pole.
So, when an act of sin thou leav'st undone,
'Tis because God hath shown thee what to shun.[2]

O gracious Lord, with whom disguise is vain,
Mask not our evil, let us see it plain!
But veil the weakness of our good desire,
Lest we lose heart and falter and expire.

XLIV.
UNSEEN MIRACLES[1]

Secret miracles and graces emanating from the Pīr transform the heart of the disciple;

For within the Saints there are spiritual resurrections innumerable, of which the least is this, that all nigh unto them become intoxicated with God.

If evidentiary miracles, like the Prophet's splitting of the moon, produce an immediate effect upon the soul,

'Tis because the soul is brought into touch with the Producer of the effect by means of a hidden link.

The effects which these miracles produce upon inanimate things are only accessory: their real object is invisible.

How superior is the bread made without dough—the Messiah's table of food from Heaven, Mary's fruit that never knew the orchard![2]

---

[1] *Math.* IV, 1332.

[2] Our evil thoughts and actions are the result of ignorance: they would never come into being unless they were presented to us in the form of good. God in His Wisdom lets appearances deceive us, so that we sin blindly and remain in darkness till He opens our eyes.

---

[1] *Math.* VI, 1300. Although it is the essential nature of all miracles to bestow spiritual life, knowledge, and power on those who are capable of being "converted," Rūmī makes a distinction in that respect between the evidentiary miracle (*mu'jizah*) of the prophet and the secret miracle (*karāmah*) of the saint. While the psychological effects of the *mu'jizah* are associated with a manifest breach in the world-order, the miraculous influence of the *murshid* on the *murīd* is a gift of Divine grace working invisibly and directly in the heart.

[2] Analogies for faith that is "the substance of things unseen." See *Qur'ān* III, 32 and V, 114.

XLV.
THE REWARD OF THE RIGHTEOUS[1]

At the Gathering for Judgement the Faithful will say, "O Angel, is not Hell the common road
Trodden by the believer and infidel alike? Yet we saw not any smoke or fire on our way."[2]
Then the Angel will reply: "That garden which ye saw as ye passed
Was indeed Hell, but unto you it appeared a pleasaunce of greenery.
Since ye strove against the flesh and quenched the flames of lust for God's sake,
So that they became verdant with holiness and lit the path to salvation;
Since ye turned the fire of wrath to meekness, and murky ignorance to radiant knowledge;
Since ye made the fiery soul (*nafs*) an orchard where nightingales of prayer and praise were ever singing—
So hath Hell-fire become for you greenery and roses and riches without end."

XLVI.
THE SAINT'S VISION OF ETERNITY[1]

What you see in the bright mirror—the Pīr sees more than that in the unpolished iron brick.[2]
The Pīrs are they whose spirits were in the Sea of Divine Munificence before this world existed.[3]

---

[1]*Math.* II, 2554.
[2]According to *Qur'ān* XIX, 72, all the Faithful shall enter Hell: "there is not one of you but shall go down to it"—a text which is usually interpreted as referring to the Bridge (*Ṣirāṭ*) over Hell. Cf. the Tradition that Hell will speak to the Faithful on the Day of Judgement and say: "Cross the Bridge, O true believer, for thy light hath put out my fire."

---

[1]*Math.* II, 167.
[2]The "brick" (*khisht*) is the iron plate which the polisher (*ṣaqqāl*) converts into a mirror. Where ordinary men perceive only the phenomenal aspect, the Pīr descries the real nature and character. As the organ of Divine consciousness, "he knows the entire content of past, present, and future existence, how everything came to be and is now coming and shall at last come to be: all this he knows both synthetically and analytically." (Jīlī).
[3]*i.e.* they are universal modes (*ta'ayyunāt*) of Pure Being and essentially one with the Light of Mohammed (the Logos).

They lived ages before the creation of the body; they harvested the wheat before it was sown.[4]
Before the form was moulded, they had received the spirit; before the sea was made, they had strung the pearl.
The spirit has beheld the wine in the grape, the spirit has beheld entity in non-entity—
The finite as infinite, the minted gold before the existence of the mine.

XLVII.
BEWARE OF HURTING THE SAINT[1]

O you who stab the selfless one with the sword, you are stabbing yourself with it. Beware!
For the selfless one has passed away and is safe; he dwells in safety for ever.
His form has passed away, he has become a mirror: naught is there but the image of another's face.[2]
If you spit at it, you spit at your own face; and if you strike the mirror, you strike yourself;
And if you see an ugly face in the mirror, 'tis you; and if you see Jesus and Mary, 'tis you.
He is neither this nor that: he is pure and free from self: he puts your image before you.

---

[4]The Perfect Man contemplates the final causes of things as logically prior to their objective existence.

---

[1]*Math.* IV, 2138. These lines give the moral of a story concerning Bāyazīd al-Bisṭāmī which the poet has borrowed, along with many others, from the Legend of the Moslem Saints. It is related that one day Bāyazīd, having attained to the state of "deification" cried out in ecstasy, "Glory to me! Within this mantle there is none but God." Rūmī describes the sequel:

> "His disciples, frenzied with horror, dashed their knives at his holy body,
> Like the fanatics (Assassins) of Girdakūh, they ruthlessly stabbed their spiritual Director.
> Every one who plunged a dagger in the Shaykh made a gash in his own body.
> There was no wound on the body of the Master, while the disciples were drowned in blood.
> Whoever aimed a blow at his throat saw his own throat cut and came to a miserable end."

[2]The perfect saint is the mirror of Truth, in which the real forms of all things are reflected, good as good and evil as evil. Hence the poet (II, 75) thanks God that in Ḥusāmu'l-Dīn he beholds nothing but spiritual beauty and purity. If you are an enemy to the saints, it is only because they show you the image of your hateful self.

XLVIII.
THE DISINTERESTED CADI[1]

He is God's deputy and the shadow of God's justice, the mirror that displays the true nature of every plaintiff and defendant;

For he inflicts punishment on behalf of those who have been wronged; not for honour's sake nor in anger nor for profit.

He who strikes and kills for his own sake is held responsible; he who strikes and kills for God's sake is immune.

If a father beats his undutiful son and the son die in consequence, the father must pay the blood-price,[2]

Because he beat him for his own benefit: a son is bound to serve his father.[3]

But suppose a schoolboy is flogged and dies: his teacher incurs no penalty;

For it is not the boy's duty to serve his teacher: therefore in chastising him he gains nothing for himself.[4]

The teacher is God's trustee; and the same rule applies to every trustee.[5]

Behead yourself! Whatever you do selflessly, 'tis a case of *thou didst not throw when thou threwest.*[6]

XLIX.
GOOD WORDS[1]

The mother is always seeking her child: the fundamentals pursue the derivatives.

---

[1]*Math.* VI, 1512. Here the Perfect Man is depicted as a judge invested with superhuman authority and as a trustee responsible to God alone.

[2]Abū Ḥanīfah was of this opinion.

[3]The son is bound to serve his father's interests: therefore the father's motive in correcting the faults of his son is really self-interest, and he incurs the legal penalty for manslaughter if his unsparing use of the rod has fatal results.

[4]Moslem jurists hold that a teacher, acting as the deputy of Him Who "taught Adam the Names," may inflict the most severe corporal punishment on his pupils with impunity, since the benefit in this case is entirely theirs.

[5]A trustee has no personal responsibility for unavoidable damage or destruction of property placed in his charge.

[6]See *Qur'ān* VIII, 17. In reality it was God, not the Prophet, who threw a handful of gravel in the faces of the Quraysh at Badr and caused them to flee. Ṣūfīs frequently cite this text in connexion with their doctrine of mystical self-abandonment (*fanā*).

---

[1]*Math.* I, 878. The "good words" (*al-kalim al-ṭayyiba*) are the Moslem profession of faith (*lā ilāha illā 'llāh*) and other expressions of praise and worship, used in the sense which Ṣūfīs attach to them.

If water is confined in a tank, the wind sucks it up; for the wind is an elemental spirit, powerful and free.
It frees the water and wafts it away to its source, little by little, so that you cannot see it wafting;
And our soul likewise the breath of our praise steals away, little by little, from the prison of this world.
The perfumes of our good words ascend even unto Him, ascending from us whither He knoweth.[2]
Our breaths soar up with the choice words, as a gift from us, to the abode of everlastingness;
Then comes to us the recompense of our praise, a recompense manifold, from God the Merciful;
Then He causes us to seek more good words, so that His servant may win more of His Mercy.
Verily the source of our delight in prayer is the Divine Love which without rest draws the soul home.

L.

"HERE AM I"[1]

One night a certain man cried "Allah!" till his lips grew sweet with praising Him.
The Devil said, "O man of many words, where is the response 'Here am I' (*labbayka*) to all this 'Allah'?
Not a single response is coming from the Throne: how long will you say 'Allah' with grim face?"
He was broken-hearted and lay down to sleep: in a dream he saw Khaḍir amidst the verdure,[2]
Who said, "Hark, you have held back from praising God: why do you repent of calling unto Him?"
He answered. "No 'Here am I' is coming to me in response: I fear that I am turned away from the Door."
Said Khaḍir, "Nay; God saith: That 'Allah' of thine is My 'Here am I,' and that supplication and grief

---

[2]Cf. *Qur'ān* XXXV, II.

---

[1]*Math.* III, 189. Selfless prayer arises from the presence of God in the heart and is answered before it is uttered.
[2]The mysterious holy personage known by the name of Khaḍir assumes many forms in Moslem legend. See the *Encyclopaedia of Islam*. "Verdure" in this verse alludes to his name, literally "the green man," and his association with spiritual life and growth.

And ardour of thine is My messenger to thee. Thy fear and love are the noose to catch My Favour:
Beneath every 'O Lord' of thine is many a 'Here am I' from Me."

LI.
THE SOUL OF PRAYER[1]

Jalalu'l-Dīn was asked, "Is there any way to God nearer than the ritual prayer?" "No," he replied; "but prayer does not consist in forms alone. Formal prayer has a beginning and an end, like all forms and bodies and everything that partakes of speech and sound; but the soul is unconditioned and infinite: it has neither beginning nor end. The prophets have shown the true nature of prayer. . . . Prayer is the drowning and unconsciousness of the soul, so that all these forms remain without. At that time there is no room even for Gabriel, who is pure spirit. One may say that the man who prays in this fashion is exempt from all religious obligations, since he is deprived of his reason. Absorption in the Divine Unity is the soul of prayer."[2]

LII.
THE FRIEND WHO SAID "I"[1]

A certain man knocked at his friend's door: his friend asked, "Who is there?"
He answered, "I." "Begone," said his friend, "'tis too soon: at my table there is no place for the raw."
How shall the raw one be cooked but in the fire of absence? What else will deliver him from hypocrisy?
He turned sadly away, and for a whole year the flames of separation consumed him;
Then he came back and again paced to and fro beside the house of his friend.
He knocked at the door with a hundred fears and reverences, lest any disrespectful word might escape from his lips.

---

[1]*Fīhi mā fīhi*, 15.
[2]Ṣūfīs often describe "the naughting of self-consciousness (*fanā'u 'l-ṣifāt*)" which results from intense concentration of every faculty on God in the performance of the ritual prayer (*ṣalāt*). The Prophet is said to have declared that no *ṣalāt* is complete without the inward presence of God. To him every *ṣalāt* was a new Ascension (mi'rāj), in which he left even Gabriel behind. See *Kashf al-Maḥjūb*, p. 302.

---

[1]*Math.* I, 3056. Mystical union involves a transformation of the lover's personality into that of the Beloved.

"Who is there?" cried his friend. He answered, "Thou, O charmer of all hearts!"
"Now," said the friend, "since thou art I, come in: there is no room for two I's in this house.
The double end of thread is not for the needle: inasmuch as thou art single, enter the needle."[2]
'Tis the thread that enters the needle: the needle's eye will not admit the camel.[3]
How shall the camel be fined down save by the shears of asceticism?[4]
But that, O reader, requires the Hand of God, which is the *Be and it was* of every impossibility.
Even non-existence, though more dead than the dead, must hearken when He calls it into being.
Recite the text, "*Every day He is engaged in some affair*: do not deem Him idle and inactive.[5]
His least act, every day, is that He despatches three armies:
One army from the loins of the fathers towards the mothers, in order that the plant may grow in the womb;
One army from the wombs to the Earth, that the world may be filled with male and female;
One army from the Earth to what lies beyond death, that every one may behold the beauty of good works.

LIII.
GOD BEYOND PRAISE[1]

When beams of Wisdom strike on soils and clays
Receptive to the seed, Earth keeps her trust:
In springtime all deposits she repays,
Taught by eternal Justice to be just.

---

[2]The mystic becomes "single" when he ceases to be conscious of himself as an *alter ego* beside God, who is the only real Ego.
[3]Unbelievers "will not enter Paradise till the camel passes through the needle's eye" (*Qur'ān* VII, 38). Cf. St. Matthew XIX, 24.
[4]The carnal nature is symbolized by a thorn-eating camel.
[5]*Qur'ān* LV, 29.

---

[1]*Math.* I, 508. Everything in the universe obeys and glorifies God (*Qur'ān* XVII, 46, etc.). Rūmī, like Ibnu'l-'Arabī, regards the whole inanimate creation as potentially endowed with life, perception, knowledge and reason.

O Thou whose Grace informs the witless clod,
Whose Wrath makes blind the heart and eye within,
My praise dispraises Thee, Almighty God;
For praise is being, and to be is sin.[2]

LIV.

KNOWLEDGE IS POWER[1]

Knowledge is the seal of the Kingdom of Solomon: the whole world is form, and knowledge is its spirit.[2]

Because of this virtue, the creatures of the seas and those of hill and plain are helpless before Man.

Of him the pard and the lion are afraid; the crocodile of the great river trembles.

From him peri and demon take refuge, each lurks in some hiding-place.

Man hath many a secret enemy: the cautious man is wise.

There are hidden beings, evil and good: at every moment their blows are falling on the heart.[3]

The pricks of angelic inspiration and satanic temptation come from thousands, not only from one.

Wait for your senses to be transmuted, so that you may discern these occult presences

And see whose words you have rejected and whom you have made your captain.

---

[2] These lines refer to the mystic's "passing away" from his praise of God through absorption in the Object of praise (*al-fanā bi-'l-Madhkūr 'ani 'l-dhikr*). So long as he is certain of existing and acting individually, he is in effect denying the Divine Unity. According to a hemistich quoted by Junayd: "thy being (*wujūduka*) is a sin with which no other sin may be compared."

---

[1] *Math.* I, 1030.

[2] The phenomenal world is the outward form of Universal Reason; its essence the Divine Knowledge that animates and rules it as the spirit animates and rules the body. Man is potentially capable of attaining to this knowledge, which may be likened to the magic seal whereby Solomon exercised dominion over men and jinn and beasts and birds.

[3] A reference to the Moslem belief that the heart (*qalb*) is a battlefield for invisible hosts of devils and guardian angels.

LV.
OUR REAL NAMES[1]

Do thou hear the name of every thing from the Knower: hear the meaning of the mystery of *He taught him the Names.*[2]
With us, the name of every thing is its outward form; with the Creator, its inward essence.
In the eyes of Moses the name of his rod was "staff"; in the eyes of God its name was "dragon."[3]
Here the name of 'Umar was "idolater"; but in eternity it was "true believer."[4]
Before God, in short, that which is our end is our real name.[5]

LVI.
IMMEDIATE KNOWLEDGE[1]

Come, recognize that your sensation and imagination and understanding are like the reed-cane on which children ride.
The spiritual man's knowledge bears him aloft; the sensual man's knowledge is a burden.
God hath said, *Like an ass laden with books:* heavy is the knowledge that is not inspired by Him;[2]
But if you carry it for no selfish ends, the load will be lifted and you will feel delight.[3]
How can you become free without the wine of Him, O you who are content with the sign of Him?

---

[1]*Math.* I, 1238.
[2]"The Knower," *i.e.* the possessor of immediate knowledge who, like Adam (*Qur'ān* II, 29), receives it from God and sees all things as they are in their essential nature.
[3]When Moses cast down his rod, it assumed the form of a dragon from which Pharaoh's magicians and followers fled in panic.
[4]'Umar, the second Caliph, before his conversion to Islam, was a violent enemy of the Prophet and a persecutor of the Faithful.
[5]St. Francis of Assisi said, "What every one is in the eyes of God, that he is, and no more."

---

[1]*Math.* I, 3445.
[2]The quotation is from *Qur'ān* LXII, 5.
[3]*i.e.* God will endow you with real knowledge.

From attribute and name what is born? Phantasy; but phantasy shows the way to the Truth.[4]

Do you know any name without a reality? Or have you ever plucked a rose from R.O.S.E.?[5]

You have pronounced the name: go, seek the thing named. The moon is in the sky, not in the water.

Would you rise beyond name and letter, make yourself entirely pure,

And behold in your own heart all the knowledge of the prophets, without book, without learning, without preceptor.

LVII.
TRADITION AND INTUITION[1]

The ear is a go-between, the eye a lover in unison with the beloved; the eye has the actual bliss, while the ear has only the words that promise it.[2]

In *hearing* there is a transformation of qualities; in *seeing*, a transformation of essence.[3]

If your knowledge of fire has been ascertained from words alone, seek to be cooked by fire!

There is no intuitive certainty until you burn: if you desire that certainty, sit down in the fire!

When the ear is subtle, it becomes an eye; otherwise, the words are enmeshed and cannot reach the heart.[4]

---

[4]Although the words denoting Divine Names and Attributes convey but a shadowy idea (*khayāl*) of His nature, yet the Ṣūfī who recites them and meditates on their meaning becomes inspired with love for their object; for every Divine Name (*ism*) is ultimately identical with the Named (*musammā*) whom it objectifies. Regarded externally it is only "the name of a name" and constitutes a "veil" (*ḥijāb*) over the essence of the Named.

[5]For the doctrine that no appearance is altogether divorced from reality, see No. XCV. "A rose from R.O.S.E.": in Persian, "*gul* from (the letters) *gāf* and *lām*."

---

[1]*Math.* II, 858.

[2]The ear plays the part of a *dallālah* (professional match-maker), whose business it is to describe a girl's beauty to the prospective bridegroom.

[3]"Hearing" (*sam'*), *i.e.* knowledge based on authority, whether oral or written, can change only the mental and moral qualities of the hearer or reader: it cannot effect that complete transformation of the "self" which is wrought by immediate vision of the Divine. In the next verses Rūmī contrasts the certainty derived from "hearing" (*'ilmu 'l-yaqīn*) with the certainty gained by seeing (*'aynu 'l-yaqīn*) and realized in actual experience (*ḥaqqu 'l-yaqīn*).

[4]The rudiments of spiritual knowledge are received through the ear, and when these ideas penetrate the heart and are apprehended by the *oculus cordis*, hearing becomes vision.

LVIII.
FEELING AND THINKING[1]

Some one struck Zayd a hard blow from behind. He was about to retaliate,
When his assailant cried, "Let me ask you a question: first answer it, then strike me.
I struck the nape of your neck, and there was the sound of a slap. Now I ask you in a friendly way—
'Was the sound caused by my hand or by your neck, O pride of the noble?'"
Zayd said, "The pain I am suffering leaves me no time to reflect on this problem.
Ponder it yourself: he who feels the pain cannot think of things like this."

LIX.
MYSTICAL PERCEPTION[1]

The five spiritual senses are linked with one another: all the five have grown from one root.[2]
The strength of one invigorates the others: each becomes a cupbearer to the rest.
Vision increases the power of speech; the inspired speech makes vision more penetrating.
Clairvoyance sharpens every sense, so that perception of the unseen becomes familiar to them all.
When one sheep has jumped over a stream, the whole flock jump across on each other's heels.
Drive the sheep, thy senses, to pasture; let them browse in the verdant meadow of Reality,
That every sense of thine may become an apostle to others and lead all their senses into that Paradise;
And then those senses will tell their secret to thine, without words and without conveying either literal or metaphorical meanings.[3]

---

[1]*Math.* III, 1380. An apologue showing the futility of intellectual speculation in the face of mystical truth.

---

[1]*Math.* II, 3236.
[2]The faculties of the soul, corresponding to the five bodily senses, are derived from the Universal Spirit and serve to manifest Divine attributes: they are not separate and distinct but involved in one another. As Edward Carpenter says, "this (mystical) perception seems to be one in which all the senses unite into one sense."
[3]The illumined saint comes as an apostle to shed light on all and guide them to the Truth. He reads their hearts by pure intuition; his knowledge is infallible, since it is not communicated to him by words, which could only be ambiguous and misleading.

LX.
LOVE AND FEAR[1]

The mystic ascends to the Throne in a moment; the ascetic needs a month for one day's journey.

Although, for the ascetic, one day is of great value, yet how should his one day be equal to *fifty thousand years*?[2]

In the life of the adept, every day is fifty thousand of the years of this world.[3]

Love (*maḥabbat*), and ardent love (*'ishq*) also, is an Attribute of God; Fear is an attribute of the slave to lust and appetite.[4]

Love hath five hundred wings, and every wing reaches from above the empyrean to beneath the earth.

The timorous ascetic runs on foot; the lovers of God fly more quickly than lightning.

May Divine Favour free thee from this wayfaring! None but the royal falcon hath found the way to the King.

LXI.
THE ASCENDING SOUL[1]

I died as mineral and became a plant,
I died as plant and rose to animal,
I died as animal and I was Man.
Why should I fear? When was I less by dying?
Yet once more I shall die as Man, to soar
With angels blest; but even from angelhood

---

[1]*Math.* V, 2180, a passage contrasting the slow and painful progress (*sulūk*) of the self-centred ascetic with the inward rapture (*jadhbah*) which in a moment carries the mystic to his goal. Cf. No. XXV, note 3.

[2]From *Qur'ān* LXX, 4: "the angels and the Spirit (Gabriel) ascend to Him on a Day whereof the span is fifty thousand years." Ṣūfīs interpret this text as a reference to the mystical resurrection and ascension.

[3]"The life of the adept" consists entirely in contemplation (*mushā-hadah*), and its "days" (*ayyāmu 'llāh*) are the infinite, timeless epiphanies (*tajalliyāt*) in which God reveals Himself to His true lovers.

[4]There is Qur'ānic authority for *maḥabbat*, but none for *'ishq*, the key-word of Ṣūfī erotic symbolism. The stronger term, however, appears in a Holy Tradition reported by Ḥasan of Basrah (*ob.* A.D. 728): "God said, 'When My servant devotes himself to praise and recollection (*dhikr*) of Me and takes delight in it, I love him and he loves Me (*'ashi-qanī wa-'ashiqtuhu*).'"

---

[1]*Math.* III, 3901. See Nos. CXVII and CXVIII.

I must pass on: *all except God doth perish.*[2]
When I have sacrificed my angel-soul,
I shall become what no mind e'er conceived.
Oh, let me not exist! for Non-existence
Proclaims in organ tones. "To him we shall return."[3]

LXII.
THE NEGATIVE WAY[1]

In the presence of the drunken Turk, the minstrel began to sing of the Covenant made in eternity between God and the soul.[2]
"I know not whether Thou art a moon or an idol, I know not what Thou desirest of me,
I know not what service to do Thee, whether I should keep silence or express Thee in words.
'Tis marvellous that Thou art Nigh unto me; yet where am I and where Thou, I know not."
In this fashion he opened his lips, only to sing "I know not, I know not."
At last the Turk leaped up in a rage and threatened him with an iron mace.
"You crazy fool!" he cried. "Tell me something you know, and if you don't know, don't talk nonsense."
"Why all this palaver?" said the minstrel, "My meaning is occult."
Until you deny all else, the affirmation of God escapes you: I am denying in order that you may find the way to affirm.
I play the tune of negation: when you die death will disclose the mystery—
Not the death that takes you into the dark grave, but the death whereby you are transmuted and enter into the Light.
O Amīr, wield the mace against yourself: shatter egoism to pieces!"

---

[2]*Qur'ān* XXVIII, 88.
[3]*Qur'ān* II, 151. For the term "non-existence" (*'adam*) applied to self-abandonment (*fanā*), see No. CXIII, note 3.

---

[1]*Math.* VI, 703.
[2]"Minstrel" probably denotes the Perfect Man teaching his disciples to follow the path of self-negation (*fanā*), not as an end in itself, but because it leads to positive and real union with God (*baqā*). In other words, mystical "intoxication" (*sukr*) should be regarded only as a prelude, and therefore relatively inferior, to "sobriety" (*saḥw*), in which the mystic rises from negation of the Many to affirmation of the One revealed in the Many. This is the true significance of the Moslem profession of faith, *lā ilāha illā 'llāh*, prefigured by the Primal Covenant (*mīthāq*) in eternity between God and all human souls: *"He brought forth from the children of Adam, from their reins, their seed, and made them testify of themselves, saying, 'Am not I your Lord.?' They answered, 'Yea, we testify.'"* See *Qur'ān* VII, 171.

LXIII.
THE SPIRIT OF THE UNIVERSE[1]

What worlds mysterious roll within the vast,
The all-encircling ocean of the Mind!
Cup-like thereon our forms are floating fast,
Only to fill and sink and leave behind
No spray of bubbles from the Sea upcast.

The Spirit thou canst not view, it comes so nigh.[2]
Drink of this Presence! Be not thou a jar
Laden with water, and its lip stone-dry;
Or as a horseman blindly borne afar,
Who never sees the horse beneath his thigh.

LXIV.
THE ABSOLUTE[1]

We and our existences are non-existent: Thou art the Absolute appearing in the guise of mortality.[2]
That which moves us is Thy Gift: our whole being is of Thy creation.
Thou didst show the beauty of Being unto not-being, after Thou hadst caused not-being to fall in love with Thee.[3]
Take not away the delight of Thy Bounty: take not away Thy dessert and wine and wine-cup!
But if Thou take it away, who will question Thee? Does the picture quarrel with the painter?
Look not on us, look on Thine Own Loving-kindness and Generosity!

---

[1]*Math.* I, 1109.
[2]Reason or Spirit, the Divine element in Man, is hidden from our perception by its immanence and the universality with which its attributes and effects are manifested.

---

[1]*Math.* I, 602. See the Introduction.
[2]Ibnu'l-'Arabī, and Rūmī after him, use the term "not-being" (*'adam* or *nīstī*) to denote things which, though non-existent in one sense, are existent in another: *e.g.*: the external world, which exists as a form but not as an essence, and the intelligible world, which exists as a concept but not as a form.
[3]Here "not-being" signifies "relative non-existence," and is applied to the world existing potentially as an idea in God's knowledge before the latent realities (*a'yān-i thābitah*) of all things were brought into actual and objective existence. God caused this "not-being" to love Him, *i.e.* by His grace every "reality" (*'āyn-i thābitah*) or potentiality was made capable (= desirous) of receiving the concrete existence which He bestowed upon it.

We were not: there was no demand on our part; yet Thy Grace heard our silent prayer and called us into existence.[4]
In the Divine court of audience all are helpless as tapestry before the needle.
Now He makes a portrait of the Devil, now of Adam; now He depicts joy, now sorrow.
None can raise a hand in defence; none dare utter a word concerning injury or benefit.

LXV.
FONS VITAE[1]

Poor copies out of Heaven's original,
Pale earthly pictures mouldering to decay,
What care although your beauties break and fall,
When that which gave them life endures for aye?

Oh, never vex thine heart with idle woes:
All high discourse enchanting the rapt ear,
All gilded landscapes and brave glistering shows
Fade—perish, but it is not as we fear.

Whilst far away the living fountains ply,
Each petty brook goes brimful to the main.
Since brook nor fountain can for ever die,
Thy fears how foolish, thy lament how vain!

What is this fountain, wouldst thou rightly know?
The Soul whence issue all created things.
Doubtless the rivers shall not cease to flow
Till silenced are the everlasting springs.

Farewell to sorrow, and with quiet mind
Drink long and deep: let others fondly deem
The channel empty they perchance may find,
Or fathom that unfathomable stream.

---

[4]Existence (*wujūd*) is a Divine Gift and, like all the Gifts of God, is conferred "on request." The request (*su'āl*) may be either explicit or implicit, *i.e.* in virtue of the state or capacity of the asker, as, for example, the state of a parched plant amounts to a request for water, while a seed buried in the earth is virtually *asking* to grow and spring up. From this point of view, "everything was created at the demand of need" (*Math.* III, 3204 *seqq.*).

---

[1]*Dīwān, SP*, XII.

The moment thou to this low world wast given,
A ladder stood whereby thou mightst aspire;
And first thy steps, which upward still have striven,
From mineral mounted to the plant; then higher

To animal existence; next, the Man
With knowledge, reason, faith. O wondrous goal!
This body, which a crumb of dust began—
How fairly fashioned the consummate whole!

Yet stay not here thy journey: thou shalt grow
An angel bright and have thine home in Heaven.
Plot on, plunge last in the great Sea, that so
Thy little drop make oceans seven times seven.

"The Son of God!" Nay, leave that word unsaid;
Say, "God is One, the pure, the single Truth."
What though thy frame be withered, old, and dead,
If the soul keep her fresh immortal youth?

LXVI.
THE PURPOSE OF CREATION[1]

Divine Wisdom created the world in order that all things in His Knowledge should be revealed.

God laid upon the world the throes of parturition for the purpose of making manifest that which He knew.[2]

You cannot sit inactive for a moment, you cannot rest till some good or evil has issued from you.

All these cravings for action were ordained to the end that your inward consciousness should come clearly into sight.

How can the real, which is the body, be at rest when the thread, which is the mind, is pulling it?[3]

This world and yonder world are incessantly giving birth: every cause is a mother, its effect the child.

When the effect is born, it too becomes a cause and gives birth to wondrous effects.

These causes are generation on generation, but it needs a very well lighted eye to see the links in their chain.

---

[1]*Math.* II, 994.

[2]God has willed that the world, of which Man is the epitome, should objectify the whole content of His Knowledge. Our ceaseless activities arise from the duty of manifesting the Divine consciousness which is the ground of human nature.

[3]Since God is always working in the heart, the body cannot be idle. "The tree of Man was never quiet."

LXVII.
DIVINE PROVIDENCE[1]

Does any painter paint a beautiful picture for the sake of the picture itself?
Nay, his object is to please children or recall departed friends to the memory of those who loved them.
Does any potter mould a jug for the jug's sake and not in hope of the water?
Does any calligrapher write for the writing's sake and not for the benefit of the reader?
'Tis like moves in chess, my son: perceive the result of each move in the next one.
By discerning cause within cause, one after another, you arrive at victory and checkmate.
The man of dull spirit knows not how to advance: he acts on trust and steps forward blindly.
Blind trust, when you are engaged in war, is as vain as a gambler's reliance on his luck.[2]
When the barriers in front and behind are lifted, the eye penetrates and reads the tablet of the Invisible.
Such a clairvoyant looks back to the origin of existence—he sees the angels dispute with the Almighty as to making our Father (Adam) His vicegerent;[3]
And again, casting his eye forward, he beholds all that shall come to pass till the Day of Judgement.
Everyone sees the things unseen according to the measure of his illumination.
The more he polishes the heart's mirror, the more clearly will he descry them.
Spiritual purity is bestowed by the Grace of God; success in polishing is also His Gift.
Work and prayer depend on aspiration: *Man hath nothing but what he hath worked for.*[4]
God alone is the Giver of aspiration: no churl aspires to be a King;[5]

---

[1]*Math.* IV, 2881.
[2]In the battle against the flesh those who have no light but from their own wits inevitably lose the game.
[3]*Qur'ān* II, 28: "The Lord said to the angels, 'Lo, I am about to place a viceroy in the earth.' They said, 'Wilt Thou place therein one who will do evil and shed blood? (We are more worthy, since) we glorify Thee.' God said, 'Verily I know what ye know not.'"
[4]*Qur'ān* LIII, 40.
[5]The mystic's aspiration is the consequence and proof of his preelection.

Yet God's assignment of a particular lot to any one does not hinder him from exercising will and choice.
When trouble comes, the ill-fated man turns his back on God, while the blessed man draws nigher unto Him.

LXVIII.
CAUSATION[1]

God hath established a rule and causes and means for the sake of all who seek Him under this blue canopy.
Most things come to pass according to the rule, but sometimes His Power breaks the rule.
He established a goodly rule and custom: He made the evidentiary miracle a breach of the custom.
O thou who art ensnared by causes, do not imagine that the Causer is defunct!
The Causer brings into existence whatsoever He will, His Omnipotence can destroy all causes;
But, for the most part, He lets the execution of His Will follow the course of causation, in order that seekers may be able to pursue their object of desire.
When there is no cause, what way should the seeker pursue? He must have a visible cause in the way he is going.
Causes are films on the eyes, for not every eye is worthy to contemplate His work.
It needs a piercing eye to reach beyond the cause and remove the film entirely,
So as to behold the Causer in the spaceless world and see that all our exertion and action is mere drivel.[2]
Everything good or bad comes from the Causer: causes and means, O father, are naught
But a spectre that has appeared on the King's highway in order that the reign of ignorance may endure for a little while.

---

[1]*Math.* V, 1543. Divine Action transcends the apparent correlation of cause and effect which serves to maintain the world-order by providing a basis for human activities.

[2]This vision of the seer is not inconsistent with the view that devotional works are Divinely appointed *means* of approach to Reality (No. XXXII). What renders them worthless is our failure to discern the immediate operation of Divine Grace in creating and giving effect to them, if it be His Will so to do.

LXIX.
THE DIVINE FACTORY[1]

The Worker is hidden in the workshop: enter the workshop and behold Him!
Inasmuch as the work has woven a veil over the Worker, you cannot see Him outside of His work.[2]
The Worker dwells in the workshop: none who stays outside is aware of Him.
Come, then, into the workshop of Not-being, that you may contemplate the work and the Worker together.[3]
Pharaoh set his face towards material existence; therefore he was blind to God's workshop
And wished to alter and avert that which was eternally ordained.

LXX.
THE WORLD OF TIME[1]

Every instant thou art dying and returning. "This world is but a moment," said the Prophet.
Our thought is an arrow shot by Him: how should it stay in the air? It flies back to God.
Every instant the world is being renewed, and we unaware of its perpetual change.
Life is ever pouring in afresh, though in the body it has the semblance of continuity.[2]
From its swiftness it appears continuous, like the spark thou whirlest with thy hand.

---

[1]*Math.* II, 759.
[2]God's work is the actualization of the potential. The worker in the immaterial world perpetually clothes "not-being" with His Qualities.
[3]By dying to self (*fanā*) the mystic returns, as it were, to his pre-existent state of "not-being" as an *'ayn-i thābitah* and realizes the inseparable unity of the Divine Essence, Attributes, and Actions.

---

[1]*Math.* I, 1142. The circle of existence begins and ends in a single point, the Essence of God, which is perceived by us under the form of extension. To mystics, however, the world is "but a moment," *i.e.* a flash of Divine illumination revealing the One as the Many and the Many as the One. According to Ṣūfī and other Moslem metaphysicians, every atom of the Cosmos is continually annihilated and re-created by the immediate manifestation of Divine Energy.
[2]Cf. the saying of Heraclitus, "To him who enters the same river, other and still other waters flow."

Time and duration are phenomena produced by the rapidity of Divine Action,
As a firebrand dexterously whirled presents the appearance of a long line of fire.

LXXI.
REALITY AND APPEARANCE[1]

'Tis light makes colour visible: at night
Red, green, and russet vanish from thy sight.
So to thee light by darkness is made known:
All hid things by their contraries are shown.
Since God hath none, He, seeing all, denies
Himself eternally to mortal eyes.[2]

From the dark jungle as a tiger bright,
Form from the viewless Spirit leaps to light.
When waves of thought from Wisdom's Sea profound
Arose, they clad themselves in speech and sound.
The lovely forms a fleeting sparkle gave,
Then fell and mingled with the falling wave.
So perish all things fair, to re-adorn
The Beauteous One whence all fair things were born.

LXXII.
GOD IN NATURE[1]

The world is frozen: its name is *jamād* (inanimate): *jāmid* means "frozen," O master.
Wait till the rising of the sun of Resurrection, that thou mayst see the movement of the world's body.[2]
Since God hath made Man from dust, it behoves thee to recognize the real nature of every particle of the universe,
That while from this aspect they are dead, from that aspect they are living: silent here, but speaking Yonder.

---

[1]*Math.* I, 1121. The symbolism of light and colour comes originally from Plato.
[2]Having no object to compare and contrast with God, the mind cannot apprehend Him: it perceives only the diverse forms in which He appears.

---

[1]*Math.* III, 1008.
[2]At the Resurrection, *i.e.* when, either here or hereafter, God lets us see things as they really are, we shall know the material world in its inward aspect, which is the world of spirit and everlasting life.

When He sends them down to our world, the rod of Moses becomes a dragon in regard to us;[3]
The mountains sing with David, iron becomes as wax in his hand;[4]
The wind becomes a carrier for Solomon, the sea understands what God said to Moses concerning it.[5]
The moon obeys the sign given by Mohammed, the fire (of Nimrod) becomes a garden of roses for Abraham.[6]
They all cry, "We are hearing and seeing and responsive, though to you, the uninitiated, we are mute."
Ascend from materiality into the world of spirits, hearken to the loud voice of the universe;
Then thou wilt know that God is glorified by all inanimate things: the doubts raised by false interpreters will not beguile thee.[7]

LXXIII.
AMOR AGITAT MOLEM[1]

Love is a boundless ocean, in which the heavens are but a flake of foam.
Know that all the wheeling heavens are turned by waves of Love: were it not for Love, the world would be frozen.
How else would an inorganic thing change into a plant? How would vegetive things sacrifice themselves to become endowed with (the animal) spirit?[2]
How would (the animal) spirit sacrifice itself for the sake of that Breath by the waft whereof a Mary was made pregnant?[3]

---

[3]*Qur'ān* VII, 104 *seqq.*
[4]*Qur'ān* XXI, 79; XXXIV, 10.
[5]The wind was subject to Solomon (*Qur'ān* XXI, 81) and transported his throne from one country to another. God said to Moses, "Smite the sea with thy rod" (*Qur'ān* XXVI, 63), whereupon it opened a way for the Israelites but engulfed Pharaoh and his hosts.
[6]This verse refers to the splitting of the moon (*Qur'ān* LIV, 1) and to the miraculous preservation of Abraham (*Qur'ān* XXI, 69).
[7]According to the *Qur'ān* (XVII, 46), "there is not a thing in heaven or earth but glorifies Him." While for Ṣūfīs *taṣbīḥ-i jamādāt* is a Divinely revealed truth as well as a fact of mystical experience, Moslem rationalistic theologians explain that such praise of God can only be implicit or indirect: *e.g.* the sight of a mineral or plant may cause the person contemplating it to cry *subḥān Allāh!*

---

[1]*Math.* V, 3853.
[2]See Nos. LXI and CXVIII.
[3]The elect are inspired and regenerated by the Divine Spirit which was breathed into the Virgin Mary (*Qur'ān* XXI, 91; LXVI, 12). Cf. *Fīhi mā fīhi*, 22: "The body is like Mary, and every one of us hath a Jesus within. If the pains (of love) arise in us, our Jesus will be born." This recalls Eckhart's doctrine of the birth of Christ in the soul (Inge, *Christian Mysticism*, 162 *seq.*) and especially his saying, "The Father speaks the Word into the soul, and when the 'son' is born every soul becomes Mary."

All of them would be stiff and immovable as ice, not flying and seeking like locusts.
Every mote is in love with that Perfection and mounts upward like a sapling.
Their silent aspiration is, in effect, a hymn of Glory to God.

LXXIV.
UNIVERSAL LOVE[1]

Never, in sooth, does the lover seek without being sought by his beloved.[2]
When the lightning of love has shot into *this* heart, know that there is love in *that* heart.
When love of God waxes in thy heart, beyond any doubt God hath love for thee.
No sound of clapping comes from one hand without the other hand.
Divine Wisdom in destiny and decree made us lovers of one another.
Because of that fore-ordainment every part of the world is paired with its mate.
In the view of the wise, Heaven is man and Earth woman: Earth fosters what Heaven lets fall.
When Earth lacks heat, Heaven sends it; when she has lost her freshness and moisture, Heaven restores it.
Heaven goes on his rounds, like a husband foraging for the wife's sake;
And Earth is busy with housewiferies: she attends to births and suckling that which she bears.
Regard Earth and Heaven as endowed with intelligence, since they do the work of intelligent beings.
Unless these twain taste pleasure from one another, why are they creeping together like sweethearts?
Without the Earth, how should flower and tree blossom? What, then, would Heaven's water and heat produce?
As God put desire in man and woman to the end that the world should be preserved by their union,
So hath He implanted in every part of existence the desire for another part.
Day and Night are enemies outwardly: yet both serve one purpose,

[1]*Math.* III, 4393. Divine Love pervades the Cosmos which it created. All things, however diverse they may seem, are ruled by that essential principle and moved to work in common for its fulfilment.

[2]If Love desires Beauty, no less does Beauty desire Love: see the closing lines of the passage.

Each in love with the other for the sake of perfecting their mutual work.
Without Night, the nature of Man would receive no income, so there would be nothing for Day to spend.

The soul says to her base earthly parts, "My exile is more bitter than yours: I am celestial."
The body desires green herbs and running water, because its origin is from those;
The soul desires Life and the Living One, because its origin is the Infinite Soul.
The desire of the soul is for ascent and sublimity; the desire of the body is for pelf and means of self-indulgence;
And that Sublimity desires and loves the soul: mark the text *He loves them and they love Him.*[3]
The gist is that whenever any one seeks, the soul of the sought is desiring him;
But the lover's desire makes him haggard, while the loved one's desire makes him fair and comely.
Love, which brightens the beloved's cheek, consumes the soul of the lover.
The amber loves the straw with the appearance of wanting naught, while the straw is struggling to advance on the long road.

LXXV.
MAN THE MACROCOSM[1]

From the pure star-bright souls replenishment is ever coming to the stars of heaven.
Outwardly we are ruled by these stars, but our inward nature has become the ruler of the skies.[2]

[3]*Qur'ān* V, 59. What attracts lover to beloved and *vice versa*, and harmonizes and unites them, is nothing that exists in the phenomenal world: it is the "non-existent" Essence and Reality which mystics know by the name of Love. In the beloved it appears under the aspect of lordship and self-sufficiency, in the lover it takes the form of servitude, abasement and tribulation.

[1]*Math.* IV, 519.
[2]Heaven derives its light from the Divine Attributes which illumine the spirit of the Perfect Man. Cf. Ibn u'l-Fāriḍ: "My moon never sinks, my sun is never hidden, and all the radiant stars set their course by me."

Therefore, while in form thou art the microcosm, in reality thou art the macrocosm.[3]

Externally the branch is the origin of the fruit; intrinsically the branch came into existence for the sake of the fruit.

Had there been no hope of the fruit, would the gardener have planted the tree?

Therefore in reality the tree is born of the fruit, though it appears to be produced by the tree.

Hence Mohammed said, "Adam and all the prophets march behind me under my banner."[4]

Hence that Master of every lore uttered the mystic saying, "We are the hindmost and the foremost:"[5]

That is to say, "If seemingly I am born of Adam, yet in truth I am the ancestor of every ancestor.

Since the angels worshipped him for my sake, and he ascended to the Seventh Heaven on my account,

Therefore Father Adam was really born of me: the tree was born of the fruit.

The idea, which is first, comes last into actuality, in particular the idea that is eternal."

LXXVI.
THE PERFECT MAN[1]

The Quṭb is the lion: it is his business to hunt: all the rest eat his leavings.

---

[3]The theory of Moslem philosophers that the universe is a great Man and Man a little universe requires correction. According to Ṣūfīs, Man, though he may be regarded as a microcosm, is not a mere epitome of the universe: on the contrary, he is its origin and final cause, since it was brought into existence for his sake, and essentially the Perfect Man is the spirit of Divine Revelation through whom the whole purpose of creation is fulfilled. Cf. the verses ascribed to 'Alī:

> "Thou art the perspicuous Book whose letters unravel all mysteries.
> Thou deemest thyself a small body (microcosm), yet the greater world (macrocosm) is enfolded within thee."

[4]All the prophets were inspired by the Light of Mohammed, who (speaking as the Logos) is said to have declared that he was a prophet when Adam was clay.

[5]This Tradition asserts the superiority of Islam to Judaism and Christianity, but here Rūmī gives it a mystical turn. Mohammed, the last of the prophets in time, is the first of them in eternity.

---

[1]*Math.* V, 2339. The term *Quṭb* (Pole), as used here, denotes the Perfect Man generally and does not refer specifically to the Head of the Ṣūfī hierarchy.

So far as you can, endeavour to satisfy him, so that he may gain strength and hunt the wild beasts.[2]
When he is ailing, the people starve: all food comes from the hand of Reason.
Their spiritual experiences are only his leavings. Bear this in mind, if you desire the prey.
He is like Reason, they are as members of the body; the management of the body depends on Reason.[3]
His infirmity is of the body, not of the spirit: the weakness lies in the Ark, not in Noah.
The Quṭb revolves round himself, while round him revolve all the spheres of Heaven.
Lend some assistance in repairing his bodily ship: be his chosen slave and devoted servant.
In reality your aid is a benefit to you, not to him: God hath said, "If ye help God, ye will be helped."[4]

LXXVII.
THE WITNESS TO GOD[1]

God hath not created in the earth or in the lofty heaven anything more occult than the spirit of Man.
He hath revealed the mystery of all things, moist and dry, but He hath sealed the mystery of the spirit: "*it is of the Word of my Lord.*"[2]
Since the august eye of the Witness beheld that spirit, naught remains hidden from him.
God is named "the Just," and the Witness belongs to Him: the just Witness is the eye of the Beloved.[3]

---

[2]"Endeavour to satisfy him," *i.e.* "serve him faithfully, relieve his bodily wants, and take care not to disturb him, so that he may be left free to pursue the realities (*asrār ū ma'ānī*) which are his spiritual food. That this is what Rūmī means by "the wild beasts" cannot be doubted. Giordano Bruno in his allegory of Actaeon (*The Heroic Enthusiasts*, tr. Williams, vol. I, p. 91) not only employs the same phrase but explains it as signifying "the intelligible kinds of ideal conceptions, which are occult, followed by few, visited but rarely, and which do not disclose themselves to all those who seek them."

[3]The Quṭb, being "the form of Universal Reason," is the manager (*mudabbir*) of the world. Without his mediation, it would not be spiritually fed. See No. LXVIII.

[4]*Qur'ān* LXVII, 8.

---

[1]*Math.* VI, 2877.

[2]*Qur'ān* XVII, 87.

[3]The Perfect Man's relation to God is analogous to that of an incorruptible eye-witness whose evidence determines the judgement and thus brings into clear light the justice and other invisible qualities of the judge.

The object of God's Regard in both worlds is the pure heart: the King's gaze is fixed upon the favourite.

The mystery of His amorous play with His favourite was the origin of all the veils which He hath made.[4]

Hence our Loving Lord said to the Prophet on the night of the Ascension: "But for thee I would not have created the heavens."

LXXVIII.

THE MEDIATOR[1]

The Prophet said, "God doth not regard your outward forms: therefore in your devising seek ye the owner of the Heart."[2]

'Tis by His Favour God regards thee, not because of thy prostrations in prayer and thy almsgivings.

Since thou deemest hearts like thine to be the Heart, thou hast abandoned the search for those who possess it—

The Heart into which if seven hundred Heavens should enter, they would be lost and hidden from view.

Do not call such fragments of heart as these "the Heart": do not seek an Abū Bakr in Sabzawār![3]

The owner of the Heart is a six-faced mirror: through him God looks on all the six directions.[4]

If God reject any one, 'tis for his sake; and if He accept any one, 'tis on his authority.

God lays His Bounty on the palm of his hand, and his palm dispenses it to all objects of Divine Mercy.

The oneness of Universal Mercy with his palm is unqualified and unconditional and perfect.

---

[4]The phenomenal world was created in order that the Perfect Man might be evolved and the glory of Divine Love fully displayed in him. He, therefore, is the Beloved of God (*Ḥabību 'llāh*), a title pre-eminently belonging to Mohammed.

---

[1]*Math.* V, 869.

[2]"The owner of the Heart," *i.e.* the saint. For "heart" (*dil, qalb*) as a name for the organ of spiritual perception, cf. *oculus cordis* in Western mysticism.

[3]Here the poet alludes to a story (*Math.* V, 845 *seqq.*) concerning the people of Sabzawār (Bayhaq), who were so fanatically Shī'ite that no Sunnī could live among them.

[4]"The six directions": right, left, above, below, before, behind. The Perfect Man is "the eye of the world whereby God sees His own works" and becomes conscious of Himself in all his diverse aspects.

O rich man, if thou bring to God a hundred sacks of gold, He will say,
"Bring the Heart as a gift to My door:[5]
Bring Me the Heart that is the Pole of the world and the Soul of the soul of the soul of Adam!"

LXXIX.
ASCETICISM AND GNOSIS[1]

The gnostic is the soul of religion and piety; gnosis is the result of past asceticism.[2]
Asceticism is the labour of sowing; gnosis is the growth and harvesting of the seed.
The gnostic is both the command to do right and the right itself; both the revealer of mysteries and that which is revealed.[3]
He is our King to-day and to-morrow: the husk is for ever a slave to his goodly kernel.

LXXX.
"DIE BEFORE DEATH"[1]

The Prophet said, "O seeker of the mysteries, wouldst thou see a dead man living,
Walking on the earth, like living men; yet his spirit dwells in Heaven,
Because it has been translated before death and will not be translated when he dies—
A mystery beyond understanding, understood only by dying—
If any one wish to see a dead man walking thus visibly on the earth,

---

[5]Referring to *Qur'ān* XXVI, 88–89: "on the Day when riches and sons avail not (and none shall be helped) save him who bringeth unto God a sincere heart (*qalb salīm*)."

---

[1]*Math.* VI, 2090.
[2]"Result," *i.e.* essential substance and final cause.
[3]Since the Perfect Man unites in his consciousness all inward and outward aspects of Reality, it may be said that he is at once the Law and the Law-giver, the Mystery and the Hierophant.

---

[1]*Math.* VI, 742. The famous saying, *mūtū qabla an tamūtū,* is one of a very large number which Ṣūfīs attribute to the Prophet as evidence for their claim to have inherited his esoteric doctrine. In the following verses Rūmī paraphrases and expounds a Tradition enjoining the Faithful to imitate Abū Bakr, a type of the perfect saint dead (*fānī*) to the world and living (*bāqī*) in God. Not only Abū Bakr, but 'Umar, 'Uthmān, and 'Alī, are included among the prophets and holy men by whom the pre-existent "Light of Mohammed" is transmitted from generation to generation (*Math.* II, 905–930; cf. No. LXXXVIII).

Let him behold Abū Bakr, the devout, who in virtue of being a true witness to God became the Prince of the resurrected."[2]

Mohammed is the twice-born in this world: he died to all temporal losing and finding: he was a hundred resurrections here and now.[3]

Often they would ask him, "How long is the way to the Resurrection?"[4]

And he would answer with mute eloquence, "Does any one ask that of me who am the Resurrection?"[5]

Become the Resurrection and so behold it: becoming is the necessary condition for beholding the reality of anything.

Whether it be light or darkness, until thou become it thou wilt never know it completely.

LXXXI.
MYSTICAL DEATH AND BURIAL[1]

Thy sepulchre is not beautified by means of stone and wood and plaster;[2]

Nay, but by digging for thyself a grave in spiritual purity and burying thy egoism in His Egoism

And becoming His dust and buried in love of Him, so that His Breath may fill and inspire thee.

A tomb with domes and turrets is unpleasing to followers of the Truth.

Look now on a living man attired in satin: does the superb robe help his understanding at all?

His soul is tormented, the scorpion of anguish dwells in his sorely stricken heart.[3]

Outside, broideries and decorations; but within he is moaning, a prey to bitter thoughts;

And lo, another, wearing an old patched cloak, his thoughts sweet as the sugar-cane, his words like sugar!

---

[2]"A true witness to God": see No. LXXVII. Abū Bakr is well-known by the title of *al-Ṣiddīq*.

[3]In the Islamic world the Prophet's Ascension represents the supreme mystical experience of the "resurrected" soul which has become one with him.

[4]On being asked this question, the Prophet is said to have answered, raising his forefinger and middle finger together, "I and the Resurrection are as these twain."

[5]"With mute eloquence," literally "with the tongue of the inward state (*ḥāl*)." According to Rūmī, the Prophet did not *say* "I am the Resurrection" (cf. St John XI, 25: *ἐγώ εἰμι ἡ ἀνάστασις καὶ ἡ ζωή*) but let his essential nature speak for itself.

---

[1]*Math.* III, 130.

[2]The body resembles a tomb: to build it up and adorn it with the gauds of this world is a bad preparation for happiness hereafter.

[3]Scorpions are supposed to infest the graves of infidels and evil-doers till the Resurrection.

LXXXII.
UNITY OF SPIRIT[1]

When the rose is dead and the garden ravaged, where shall we find the perfume of the rose? In rose-water.
Inasmuch as God comes not into sight, the prophets are His vicars.
Do not mistake me! 'Tis wrong to think that the vicar and He Whom the vicar represents are two.
To the form-worshipper they are two; when you have escaped from consciousness of form, they are One.
Whilst you regard the form, you are seeing double: look, not at the eyes, but at the light which flows from them.[2]
You cannot distinguish the lights of ten lamps burning together, so long as your face is set towards this light alone.
In things spiritual there is no partition, no number, no individuals.
How sweet is the oneness of the Friend with His friends! Catch the spirit and clasp it to your bosom.
Mortify rebellious form till it wastes away: unearth the treasure of Unity!

Simple were we and all one essence: we were knotless and pure as water.[3]
When that goodly Light took shape, it became many, like shadows cast by a battlement.
Demolish the dark battlement, and all difference will vanish from amidst this multitude.[4]

LXXXIII.
CREATIONS OF PHANTASY[1]

O Thou by Whom the unspoken prayer is answered, Who bestowest at every moment a hundred bounties on the heart.

---

[1]*Math.* I, 672, a discourse on the Divine vicegerency (*Khilāfah*) of the prophets, in whom the hidden nature of God is revealed.

[2]Dualism is the result of paying attention to the outward forms of things. As the eyes are two, but their light one and indistinguishable, so the bodies of the prophets are many, but the spirit which illumines them one and the same. Moslem oculists generally adopt the theory of Galen and other Greeks that vision is produced by rays of light emitted from the eyes.

[3]Ṣūfīs identify the so-called "White Pearl," the spiritual essence of Man and original substance of all created things, with the Light of Mohammed (Universal Reason, the Logos).

[4]"The dark battlement" typifies the wall of selfhood and illusion, to which the "shadows" of plurality owe their existence.

---

[1]*Math.* V, 309.

Thou hast limned some letters of writing: rocks here become soft as wax for love of them.[2]

Thou hast scribed the *nūn* of the eyebrow, the *ṣād* of the eye and the *jīm* of the ear as a distraction to our minds and understandings.[3]

By those letters of Thine the intellect is made to weave subtle coils of perplexity: write on, O accomplished Fair-writer!

Incessantly Thou shapest beauteous forms of phantasy upon the page of Non-existence.

On the tablet of phantasy Thou inscribest wondrous letters—eye and profile and cheek and mole.

I am drunken with desire for Non-existence, not for the existent, because the Beloved of the world of Non-existence is more faithful.[4]

Behold how the madmen dote on the blackness of those lines traced without fingers!

Everyone is infatuated with a phantasy and digs in corners for the buried treasure.

One goes into church to perform religious exercises; another in his greed for gain betakes himself to sowing;

One loses his soul in the invocation of demons; another sets his foot upon the stars.

To the seeing eye it is manifest that all variety of action in the external world arises from phantasies within.

Since the object of the soul's quest is hidden, every one looks for it in a different quarter, like travellers seeking the *qiblah* in the dark.

At dawn, when the Ka'bah becomes visible, they find out who has lost his way.[5]

---

[2]The Platonist, William Drummond, uses the same analogy:

"Those golden letters which so brightly shine
In Heaven's great volume gorgeously divine,
The wonders all in sea, in earth, in air
Be but dark pictures of that sovereign Fair."

[3]The Arabic letters *ṣād, nūn, and jīm* resemble in shape the eye, the eyebrow, and the ear respectively. Viewed in its proper light, everything in the world is good. But where mystics, contemplating these "fair copies," whether sensible or ideal, perceive only the revelation of Eternal Beauty in ever-changing forms of "new creation," other men see and pursue mere shadows of their selfish selves.

[4]"Non-existence," *i.e.* Reality as opposed to phenomenality.

[5]As a rule, the ritual prayer (*ṣalāt*) is invalidated by facing in the wrong direction, but should the worshipper, owing to darkness or any other sufficient cause, fail to turn towards the Ka'bah, he does not lose the merit of his prayers, provided that he has endeavoured to the best of his judgement and ability to ascertain the direction as exactly as possible. Similarly all seek the One True Light (No. CIV). Doubt, perplexity, and error arise from ignorance.

LXXXIV.
THE MAGIC OF LOVE[1]

Love and fancy create a thousand forms beautiful as Joseph: in sooth they are greater sorcerers than Hārūt and Mārūt.[2]
Before your eyes they raise up the phantom of the Beloved: you are enraptured with it and tell it all your secrets.
'Tis as when a mother, at the grave of her child newly dead,
Speaks to him earnestly and intensely: crazed with grief, she imagines his dust to be living
And in her heart believes he is listening to her. Lo, the magic wrought by Love!
Fondly and with tears she lays her lips, time after time, on the fresh earth of the grave in such wise
As, during his life, she never laid them on the face of the son who was so dear to her.
But love for the dead does not last: when some days have passed in mourning, the flame of her grief sinks to rest.
Love has carried off his enchantments and gone away: the fire is out, only ashes remain.

LXXXV.
PHENOMENA THE BRIDGE TO REALITY[1]

The Christian confesses to his priest a year's sins—fornication and malice and hypocrisy—
In order that the priest may pardon him, for he deems the priest's absolution to be forgiveness from God.
The priest has no real knowledge of sin and pardon; but love and faith are mighty spells.

---

[1]*Math.* V, 3260.
[2]Two fallen angels who taught mankind the arts of magic. Presuming themselves to be immaculate, they had refused to do homage to Adam, so God sent them down to the earth, where they fell in love with a beautiful woman and tried to seduce her. She would not yield until they taught her the word of power that enabled them to ascend to Heaven. Having learned it, she ascended, and God transformed her into Zuhrah (the planet Venus). Hārūt and Mārūt were imprisoned in a pit at Babylon, choosing to expiate their sin in this world rather than suffer everlasting torment hereafter. The legend may be regarded as an allegory of the human spirit and reason, which descend from the World of Light to the World of Nature, fall a prey to the defilements of the flesh (*nafs*), and finally, having been purged by suffering, return to where they belong.

---

[1]*Math.* V, 3257 and 3277.

In the hour of absence Love fashions many a form of phantasy; in the hour of presence the Formless One reveals Himself,

Saying, "I am the ultimate origin of sobriety and intoxication: the beauty in all forms is reflected from Me.

Now, because thou hast often gazed on My reflexion, thou art able to contemplete My Pure Essence."

As soon as the Christian feels the pull from Yonder, he becomes unconscious of the priest.

At that moment he craves forgiveness for his trespasses from the Grace of God behind the veil.

When a fountain gushes from a rock, the rock disappears in the fountain.

LXXXVI.
THE PEAR-TREE OF ILLUSION[1]

This pear-tree is the primal egoism and self-existence that makes the eye distorted and squinting.

When thou comest down, O climber, thy thoughts and words and eyes will no more be awry.

Because of the humility shown by thee in coming down, God will endow thee with true vision.

Thou wilt see that this pear-tree has become a tree of fortune, its boughs reaching to the Seventh Heaven.

Afterwards climb up again into the tree transformed by Divine Mercy.

Now it is luminous like the Burning Bush: it cries, "*Lo, I am God!*"[2]

Beneath its shade all thy wants are satisfied: such is the Divine Alchemy.

Thy personality and existence are now lawful to thee, since thou beholdest therein the attributes of the Almighty.

The crooked tree has become straight, God-revealing: *its root in the earth, its branches in the sky.*[3]

---

[1]*Math.* IV, 3562. Boccaccio (*Decameron*, Day vii, Novel 9) and Chaucer in *The Merchant's Tale* relate how a gallant, by climbing a pear-tree and pretending that it caused hallucinations, persuaded the foolish husband to believe in his wife's innocence, though he had witnessed her misbehaviour with his own eyes. Rūmī's version of the story is given in the preceding couplets (3544–3557). Here he draws out of it a mystical application—the soul's "climb-down" from self-consciousness and ascent to God-consciousness—which goes far to justify his sometimes very broad interpretation of the maxim that every jest has a moral.

[2]See *Qur'ān* XXVIII, 29–30, and cf. Exodus III, 1–6.

[3]*Qur'ān* XIV, 29.

LXXXVII.
COSMIC CONSCIOUSNESS[1]

Wine in ferment is a beggar suing for our ferment; Heaven in revolution is a beggar suing for our consciousness.
Wine was intoxicated with us, not we with it; the body came into being from us, not we from it.
We are as bees, and bodies as the honeycomb: we have made the body, cell by cell, like wax.[2]

LXXXVIII.
THE UNIVERSAL SPIRIT REVEALED IN PROPHETS AND SAINTS[1]

Every moment the robber Beauty rises in a different shape, ravishes the soul and disappears.
Every instant the Loved One assumes a new garment, now of eld, now of youth.
Now He plunged into the heart of the potter's clay—the Spirit plunged like a diver.[2]
Anon, rising from the depths of clay that is moulded and baked, He appeared in the world.
He became Noah, and went into the Ark when at His prayer the world was flooded.
He became Abraham and appeared in the midst of the fire, which bloomed with roses for His sake.[3]
For a while He was roaming on the earth to pleasure Himself;
Then He became Jesus and ascended to Heaven and glorified God.
In brief, it was He that was coming and going in every generation thou hast known,
Until at last He appeared in the form of an Arab and gained the empire of the world.

---

[1]*Math.* I, 1811. Here the poet speaks as one of the God-intoxicated souls which live in union with the Logos and therefore may claim to be the archetype and animating principle of the universe.

[2]As bees by Divine inspiration (*Qur'ān* XVI, 70–71) build up honeycombs, so the Spirit of the Perfect Man makes the world an image of itself and fills all bodies, according to the capacity of each, with sweetness and light and knowledge and love of God.

---

[1]*Dīwān, Tab.*, 199.

[2]The Divine Spirit was breathed into the clay body of Adam, which God had kneaded with His own hands for forty days.

[3]See No. LXXII, note 6.

There is no transmigration, nothing is transferred. The lovely Winner of hearts
Became a sword in the hand of 'Alī and appeared as the Slayer of the time.[4]
No, no! 'Twas even He that cried in human shape, "*Ana 'l-Ḥaqq.*"
The one who mounted the scaffold was not Manṣūr, as the foolish imagined.[5]
Rūmī hath not spoken and will not speak words of infidelity: do not disbelieve him!

LXXXIX.

THE STANDARD-BEARERS OF DIVINE REVELATION[1]

The eternal Will and Decree of God, the Forgiver, to reveal and manifest Himself
Invokes opposition, for otherwise nothing can be shown; and there is no contrary to that incomparable King.[2]
Therefore He made a viceroy whose heart should be a mirror for His Sovereignty,
And endowed him with infinite purity, and then set up against him a dark foil.
He made two banners, white and black: one was Adam, the other was Iblīs.
Between these mighty hosts there was combat and strife, and there came to pass what was destined to come.
Likewise in the next period Abel arose, and Cain became the antagonist of his pure light.
So, from age to age and from generation to generation, the same banners were raised in conflict,
Till the advent of Mohammed, who strove with Abū Jahl, the prince of the armies of iniquity.

---

[4]Here Rūmī explicitly warns the reader against confusing a monistic doctrine with the heresy of those who believe in the transmigration of individual souls (*tanāsukh*). In another passage (*Dīwān*, Lucknow ed., p. 222) he declares that all forms in which the One Essence clothes itself are "different bottles of the same Wine," and "this," he says, "is not transmigration: it is the doctrine of Pure Unity" (*īn nīst tanāsukh, sukhun-i waḥdat-i ṣirf-ast*).

[5]"Manṣūr" refers to Ḥallāj (Ḥusayn ibn Manṣūr) executed at Baghdad in A.D. 922. He expressed his mystical relation to God in the emphatic formula *Ana 'l-Ḥaqq*, "I am God," but he would not have endorsed Rūmī's interpretation of it. Cf. No. CXV.

---

[1]*Math.* VI, 2151.

[2]The manifestation of God in the world evokes the appearance of contrariety; hence in successive ages His Beautiful and Terrible Attributes are personified and displayed as antagonists contending for mastery, though *essentially* they are one as He is One.

XC.
THE MYSTERY OF EVIL[1]

Both Moses and Pharaoh were worshippers of the Truth, though in appearance the former has found the way and the latter has lost it.[2]
In the daytime Moses was crying to God: at midnight Pharaoh would begin to moan,[3]
Saying, "O Lord, what shackle is this on my neck? Were there no shackle, who would say 'I am I'?[4]
By that decree whereby Thou hast made Moses to be illumined, by that same decree Thou hast made me to be darkened.
Both of us are fellow-slaves to Thee; but Thy axe is cleaving the sappy boughs in Thy forest.
The boughs are helpless against the axe: one it grafts firmly, another is left uncared for.
I beseech Thee, by the might of Thine axe, to show mercy and straighten my crookedness."
Once more Pharaoh said to himself in amazement, "Am not I praying all night long?
Within I am humble and obedient: how do I appear so changed when I meet with Moses?"[5]
Since colourlessness became captive to colour, a Moses came into conflict with a Moses.

---

[1]*Math.* I, 2447.

[2]Pharaoh no less than Moses serves the purpose for which he was created. It follows that *sub specie aeternitatis* all souls are ultimately saved.

[3]Moses worshipped God openly. Pharaoh, on the other hand, while proclaiming his own divinity in public, secretly acknowledged his absolute dependence on the Almighty, *i.e.* his original nature testified that he was a "vessel of wrath" and that his impiety was in accord with the inscrutable Divine Will and Knowledge concerning him.

[4]Early Ṣūfī authors quote the saying (repeated by Eckhart), "None but God has the right to say 'I'."

[5]Pharaoh's actions faithfully reflected his nature and character as it existed potentially in the Divine Mind, so that in essence there was complete harmony between him and God; he only became hostile when confronted with Moses, who represents the Command (*amr*) of God as revealed to the prophets and embodied in the religious law. What God *commands* is entirely good; but what He *wills* includes all "good" and "evil," though nothing is really evil in relation to Him.

When you attain unto the colourlessness which you had originally, Moses and Pharaoh are at peace with one another.[6]

If you ask me to explain this mystery, I reply that the world of colour cannot be devoid of opposition.

The marvel is that colour sprang from that which is without colour: how did colour arise to war with the colourless?

Or is it not really war? Is it for Divine ends—an artifice like the bickering of ass-dealers?[7]

Or is it neither this nor that? Is it sheer bewilderment? The treasure must be sought, and bewilderment is the ruin where it lies buried.[8]

What you conceive to be the treasure—any such conception causes you to lose the real treasure.

Fancies and opinions are like the state of cultivation: treasure is not found in cultivated spots.

In the state of cultivation there is existence and contrariety: the Non-existent spurns everything that exists.[9]

XCI.
THE LAW AND THE TRUTH[1]

Yesterday a man who was fond of dialectic put a question to me.

He said, "The Prophet says that to be pleased with infidelity is an act of infidelity; and his words are conclusive, like a seal.

But he has also declared that the Moslem must be pleased with every Divine Ordainment.

---

[6]"Colourlessness," the realm of pure being and absolute unity, in which there is no "colour," *i.e.* individualization (*ta'ayyun*) or limitation of any kind. Cf. Shelley:

"Life, like a dome of many-coloured glass,
Stains the white radiance of eternity."

"Colour" also suggests the dyeing-vat of Destiny and the various characters that emerge from it. When the one appears as the Many, "a Moses comes into conflict with a Moses," *i.e.* the Unity displays itself in forms which, though outwardly opposed, are in fact nothing but the Divine Essence viewed under the aspect of "otherness" and, like water and ice, ultimately identical.

[7]Does not all this show of discord mark a deep design and harmonious purpose? Wrangling ass-dealers are engaged in a conspiracy to deceive the customer and incite him to buy.

[8]Or, again, is the creation of the world a riddle insoluble by the intellect? May not the key be found in mystical bewilderment? Treasures are buried in ruins: the treasure of Divine Unity (*tawḥīd*) is discovered only by those "unbuilt from the creature" (Suso), "denuded (*verwueste*) of all attributes, empty (*wueste*) of themselves and of all things" (Eckhart).

[9]"The Non-existent," *i.e.* the formless Reality.

---

[1]*Math.* III, 1362.

Now, is not infidelity and hypocrisy God's Ordainment? If I am pleased with infidelity, I shall be disobeying God,
And if I am not pleased, that too will be wicked: how can I escape from this dilemma?"
I replied, "Infidelity is the thing ordained: not the Ordainment, but the effect of the Ordainment.[2]
I acquiesce in infidelity in that respect that it is God's Ordainment, not in this respect that it is our rebelliousness and wickedness.
In respect of the Ordainment, infidelity is not infidelity. Do not call God "infidel," recant!
Infidelity is ignorance, and the Ordainment of infidelity is wisdom: how, pray, should *ḥilm* (ruth) and *khilm* (wrath) be identical?
The ugliness of the script is not the ugliness of the scribe; nay, 'tis an exhibition of the ugly by him.
The power of the artist is shown by his ability to make both the ugly and the beautiful.
If I develop this topic, so that question and answer become lengthy,
The savour of Love's mystery will go from me, the fair form of Piety will be disfigured.

XCII.
THE COMPLETE ARTIST[1]

He is the source of evil, as thou sayest,
Yet evil hurts Him not. To make that evil
Denotes in Him perfection. Hear from me
A parable. The heavenly Artist paints
Beautiful shapes and ugly: in one picture
The loveliest women in the land of Egypt
Gazing on youthful Joseph amorously;
And lo, another scene by the same hand,
Hell-fire and Iblīs with his hideous crew:

---

[2]Acceptance of the Divine Decree (*qaḍā*) does not necessitate acceptance of the thing decreed (*maqḍī*). It is true that all sins are decreed by God; but He decrees them *quâ* actions, all of which in their essential nature proceed from Himself and are approved by Him, *not* as objects of condemnation on religious grounds. There is only an apparent conflict between His *creative* command, which brings every action into existence, and His *religious* command, which qualifies some actions as good and others as evil. The religious command is really a trial of faith and may be either obeyed or disobeyed. Therefore, while we are bound to condemn what is sinful in the eyes of the Law, we must at the same time acknowledge that God decrees and creates what, though He and we call it "sin," is in perfect unison with His Eternal Wisdom and Providence.

---

[1]*Math.* II, 2535.

Both master-works, created for good ends,
To show His Perfect Wisdom and confound
The sceptics who deny His Mastery.
Could He not evil make, He would lack skill:
Therefore He fashions infidel alike
And Moslem true, that both may witness bear
To Him, and worship One Almighty Lord.[2]

XCIII.
THE NECESSARY FOIL[1]

Privation and defect, wherever seen,
Are mirrors of the beauty of all that is.
The bone-setter, where should he try his skill
But on the broken limb? The tailor where?
Not, surely, on the well-cut finished coat.
Were no base copper in the crucible,
How could the alchemist his craft display?

XCIV.
THE RELATIVITY OF EVIL[1]

There is no absolute evil in the world: evil is relative. Recognize this fact.
In the realm of Time there is nothing that is not a foot to one and a fetter to another.
To one a foot, to another a fetter; to one a poison, to another sweet and wholesome as sugar.
Snake-venom is life to the snake, but death to man; the sea is a garden to sea-creatures, but to the creatures of earth a mortal wound.
Zayd, though a single person, may be a devil to one and an angel to another:
If you wish him to be kind to you, then look on him with a lover's eye.

---

[2]While the Divine Beauty and Mercy reflected in the nature of true believers cause them to worship God for love's sake, infidels are dominated by His Majesty and Wrath and only against their will confess themselves to be His slaves (*'ibād*).

---

[1]*Math.* I, 3201. The nature of everything is made manifest by contrast with something else that lacks its qualities. Were there no appearance of darkness and evil, we should be ignorant of light and good. To be conscious of deficiency is the first step towards perfection.

---

[1]*Math.* IV, 65.

Do not look on the Beautiful with your own eye: behold the Sought with the eye of the seeker.
Nay, borrow sight from Him: look on His face with His eye.
God hath said, "Whoso belongs to Me, I belong to him: I am his eye and his hand and his heart."
Everything loathly becomes lovely when it leads you to your Beloved.[2]

XCV.
THE SOUL OF GOODNESS IN THINGS EVIL[1]

Fools take false coins because they are like the true.
If in the world no genuine minted coin
Were current, how would forgers pass the false?
Falsehood were nothing unless truth were there,
To make it specious. 'Tis the love of right
Lures men to wrong. Let poison but be mixed
With sugar, they will cram it into their mouths.
Oh, cry not that all creeds are vain! Some scent
Of truth they have, else they would not beguile.
Say not, "How utterly fantastical!"
No fancy in the world is all untrue.
Amidst the crowd of dervishes hides one,
One true fakir. Search well and thou wilt find!

XCVI.
THE UNSEEN POWER[1]

We are the flute, our music is all Thine;
We are the mountain echoing only Thee;
Pieces of chess Thou marshallest in line
And movest to defeat or victory;

[2]In this and the preceding verse the poet refers to three Traditions. He who gives himself up entirely to God (in *fanā*) is united with Him (in *baqā*). "Paradise is encompassed with things we like not," *i.e.* we must pass through tribulations in order to reach it.

[1]*Math.* II, 2928. Error, falsehood and all evil is relative in so far as it serves to make truth and goodness manifest and is sought, not for itself, but only because it is mistaken for good. Cf. the argument of Socrates (*Meno* 77, tr. Jowett): "They do not desire the evils, who are ignorant of their nature, but they desire what they suppose to be goods although they are really evils; and if they are mistaken and suppose the evils to be goods, they really desire goods."

[1]*Math.* I, 599.

Lions emblazoned high on flags unfurled—[2]
Thy wind invisible sweeps us through the world.

XCVII.

MORAL RESPONSIBILITY[1]

If we let fly an arrow, the action is not ours: we are only the bow, the shooter of the arrow is God.
This is not compulsion (*jabr*): it is Almightiness (*jabbārī*) proclaimed for the purpose of making us humble.[2]
Our humbleness is evidence of Necessity, but our sense of guilt is evidence of Free-will.
If we are not free, why this shame? Why this sorrow and guilty confusion and abashment?
Why do masters chide their pupils? Why do minds change and form new resolutions?
You may argue that the asserter of Free-will ignores God's Compulsion, which is hidden like the moon in a cloud;
But there is a good answer to that: hearken, renounce unbelief, and cleave to the Faith!
When you fall ill and suffer pain, your conscience is awakened, you are stricken with remorse and pray God to forgive your trespasses.
The foulness of your sin is shown to you, you resolve to come back to the right way;
You promise and vow that henceforth your chosen course of action will be obedience.
Note, then, this principle, O seeker: pain and suffering make one aware of God; and the more aware one is, the greater his passion.[3]
If you are conscious of God's Compulsion, why are you not heartbroken? Where is the sign of your feeling the chains with which you are loaded?

---

[2]This was a sight the poet must often have witnessed during his residence at Qoniyah. Banners and coins bearing the device of a lion surmounted by a sun are associated with the Seljūq dynasties of 'Irāq and Asia Minor.

---

[1]*Math.* I, 616. Rūmī defends the orthodox Moslem doctrine that "the creature does not create his actions and is not forced: God creates these actions together with the creature's having a free choice (*ikhtiyār*) in them."
[2]God calls Himself the Compeller (*al-Jabbār*) in order to remind us that we are His slaves and entirely subject to His Will.
[3]Suffering causes the sinner to repent, and true penitence implies self-abandonment, *i.e.* knowledge and love of God. Hence the Necessitarian, if he were really conscious of being "compelled," would turn to God in anguish and supplication like a distraught lover.

How should one make merry who is bound in chains? Does the prisoner behave like the man who is free?
Whatever you feel inclined to do, you know very well that you can do it;
But in the case of actions that you dislike, you have become a Necessitarian, saying, "Such is God's Decree."
The prophets are Necessitarians as regards the works of this world; the infidels are Necessitarians as regards the works of the world hereafter.

XCVIII.
"WHATSOEVER GOD WILLS SHALL COME TO PASS"[1]

This does not mean that you may be slack in serving God; nay, 'tis an incitement to eager exertion and entire self-devotion.
Suppose you knew that the will of such and such a vizier is law and his munificence unbounded,
Would you pay court to him with the zeal of a hundred men, or would you flee from him and his palace?
Likewise the Prophet's saying, "The Pen has dried," when you interpret it in its true sense, is a summons to the most important work of all.
If you do iniquity, you are damned: the Pen has dried on that. If you act righteously, you will eat the fruit of blessedness: the Pen has dried on that.
Is it conceivable that because of the Decree in eternity God should say, like a minister dismissed from office,
"The affair has gone out of My hands: 'tis vain to approach Me with entreaties"?
Nay, if your orisons exceed those of another by a single mite, that mite will be weighed in God's scales.[2]

XCIX.
PREDESTINATION AND FREE-WILL[1]

A Moslem called a Magian to accept the Faith of the Prophet. He replied, "I shall do so, if God will."

---

[1]*Math.* V, 3111.
[2]Cf. *Qur'ān* XCIX, 7.

---

[1]*Math.* V, 2912. In the long-drawn debate from which a few extracts are given here, the Magian upholds absolute necessitarianism, while the Moslem declares such a doctrine to be absurd.

"God wills it," said the Moslem; "but your carnal soul and the wicked Devil are dragging you to infidelity and the fire-temple."
"Well," he answered, "if they are the stronger, must not I go in the direction whither they pull me?
You say that God desires me to profess Islam: what is the use of His Desire when He cannot fulfil it?
According to you, the Flesh and the Devil have carried their will to success, while the gracious Divine Purpose has been defeated and pulverized.[2]
God forbid! Whatsoever He wills shall come to pass. He is the Ruler over the worlds of space and spacelessness.
Without His Command no one in His Kingdom shall add so much as the tip of a single hair.
The Kingdom is His, the Command is His: that Devil of His is the meanest dog at His door."

"Beyond doubt," replied the Moslem, "we possess a certain power of choice: you cannot deny the plain evidence of the inward sense.
There is such a power of choice in regard to injustice and wrong-doing: that is what I meant when I spoke of the Flesh and the Devil.[3]
The instinct to choose is latent in the soul, and sight of the desired object brings it into action.
When Iblīs shows to you an object of desire, the sleeping power awakes and moves towards it,
While, on the other hand, the Angel sets before you good objects of desire and commends them to your heart,
In order that the power to resist evil and choose good may be stimulated."
In the eyes of reason, Necessitarianism (*jabr*) is worse than the doctrine of absolute free-will (*qadar*), because the Necessitarian is denying his own consciousness.[4]

---

[2]The same argument was used by an eminent Ṣūfī, Abū Sulaymān Dārānī (*ob.* A.D. 830), against the Qadarites and Mu'tazilites: "they have made themselves and the Devil stronger than God; for they say that He created His creatures to obey Him and that Iblīs converted them to disobedience. Thus they maintain that when they will a thing it comes to pass, but when God wills a thing it does not come to pass."

[3]Although the Moslem, speaking the language of religion, attributed the Magian's infidelity to these evil forces, he did not mean that their operation is irresistible: on the contrary, it is limited by a faculty in man which enables him to choose whether or no he will accept the temptation offered to him.

[4]The existence of that which is beyond perception can more reasonably be denied than the existence of that which is perceived by the outward or inward senses. Consequently, from this point of view, the Jabrī, who denies his manifest power of choice (*ikhtiyār*) is worse than the Qadarī (Mu'tazilite), who denies the invisible Divine action.

The other does not deny this, he denies the action of the Almighty: he says, "There is smoke, but no fire."[5]
The Necessitarian sees the fire plainly: it burns his raiment, and like the sceptic he argues that it is naught.[6]

"If none but God has the power of choice, why are you angry with a thief who steals your property?
Even animals recognize this inward sense: a camel, cruelly beaten, attacks the driver; his fury is not directed against the cudgel.
The entire *Qur'ān* consists of commands and prohibitions and threats of punishment: are these addressed to stones and brickbats?
You have removed from God the possibility of impotence, but you have virtually called Him ignorant and stupid.
The doctrine of Free-will does not imply Divine impotence; and even if it did, ignorance is worse than impotence.
God's universal power of choice brought our individual power into existence: His Power is like a horseman hidden by the dust which he raises;
But His control of our acts of free-will does not deprive them of that quality.
Declare that God's Will is exercised in a complete manner, yet without imputing to Him compulsion (*jabr*) and responsibility for disobedience to His Commands.
You say your unbelief is willed by Him: know that it is also willed by yourself;
For without your will it cannot exist at all: involuntary unbelief is a self-contradiction.
Endeavour to gain inspiration from God's cup of love: then you will become selfless and without volition.
Then all volition will belong to that Wine, and you will be absolutely excusable."

C.
THE WINE OF LOVE[1]

He comes, a Moon whose like the sky ne'er saw, awake or dreaming,
Crowned with eternal flame no flood can lay.
Lo, from the flagon of Thy love, O Lord, my soul is swimming,
And ruined all my body's house of clay.

[5]*i.e.* he perceives the effect (*athar*), namely his free-will, but imputes it to himself, ignoring the Creator and Producer of the effect (*Mu'aththir*), on Whose Will his choice of good or evil ultimately depends.
[6]The Jabrī is a thorough-going sceptic, for he contradicts a universal fact of human consciousness.

[1]*Dīwān*, *SP.* VII.

When first the Giver of the grape my lonely heart befriended,
Wine fired my bosom and my veins filled up;
But when His image all my eye possessed, a voice descended:
"Well done, O sovereign Wine and peerless Cup!"

Love's mighty arm from roof to base each dark abode is hewing
Where chinks reluctant catch a golden ray.
My heart, when Love's sea of a sudden burst into its viewing,
Leaped headlong in, with "Find me now who may!"

As, the sun moving, clouds behind him run,
All hearts attend thee, O Tabrīz's Sun!

CI.

THE RIDDLES OF GOD[1]

Whosoever is perplexed and sorely troubled, God hath whispered a riddle into his ear,
That He may enmesh him in two doubtful thoughts— "Shall I do what He tells me or shall I not?"
By God's Decree one of these alternatives tilts the scale, and he adopts it.
Wouldst thou have a mind untroubled, do not stuff thy spiritual ear with cotton-wool,
So that thou mayest understand His riddles and read both the covert sign and the overt.
Then upon thine ear will descend revelation (*waḥy*). What is *waḥy*? A voice inaudible to sense-perception.[2]
The word "compulsion" (*jabr*) makes me impatient for Love's sake: 'tis only he that loves not that is fettered by compulsion.
This is communion with God, not compulsion: the shining of the moon, not a cloud:
Or, if it be compulsion, it is not ordinary compulsion: it is not the compulsion exerted by self-will, inciting us to sin.
O son, they alone know the true meaning of compulsion in whom God hath opened the heart's eye.[3]

---

[1]*Math.* I, 1456.

[2]Here and elsewhere Rūmī abolishes the orthodox distinction between the superior inspiration of prophets (*waḥy*) and the inferior of saints (*ilhām*).

[3]"Compulsion" (*jabr*), as generally understood, implies conflict of two wills and subjugation of the weaker. In this sense the term is anathema to Ṣūfīs who know and love God and, in selfless union (*ma'iyyah*) with His Will, feel perfectly free. The blissful experience of living under Divine Control may, however, be described technically as "laudable compulsion" (*jabr-i maḥmūd*).

CII.
THE APOLOGY OF IBLĪS[1]

At first I was an angel: with all my soul I trod the Way of devotion to the service of God.
How should one's first calling be forgotten? How should the first love fade away from one's heart?
Was it not the hand of His Bounty that saved me? Was it not He that raised me up from non-existence?
Who found milk for me in my infancy? Who rocked my cradle? He.
The nature that flows in with the milk—can it ever be expelled?
Bounty and Grace and Favour are the real substance of His coin, Wrath but a speck of alloy on it.
I regard not His Wrath, which is a temporary cause: I am regarding His eternally precedent Mercy.[2]
Grant that envy was the motive of my refusal to bow down before Adam; yet that envy arose from love of God, not from disobedience.
All envy arises from love, for fear lest another become the companion of the beloved.
Brooding jealousy is the inevitable consequence of love, just as "Live Long!" must follow the sneeze.[3]
Since there was no move but this on His chessboard and He bade me play, what else could I do?[4]
I played the one play that there was and cast myself into woe.
Even in woe I taste His delights: I am mated by Him, mated by Him, mated by Him!"[5]

---

[1]*Math.* II, 2617. On the theme of this passage, see Massignon, *La Passion d'al-Hallāj*, pp. 864–867 and *The Idea of Personality in Ṣūfism*, pp. 31–33. Iblīs depicts himself as the devoted lover whose jealousy forbids him to pay homage to a rival. In reality, he says, his refusal to glorify Adam was a declaration that he would worship none but God. He would suffer damnation rather than compromise the Divine Unity. Since his original nature was good, his disobedience can only be a transient lapse from grace.

[2]According to the Holy Tradition, "My Mercy preceded (or 'prevailed over') My Wrath."

[3]"Live long," *dīr zī*. Cf. Greek ζῆθι Latin *salve*. The usual Moslem formulas are "God be praised!" (*al-ḥamd lillāh*) and "God have mercy on you" (*yarḥamuk Allāh*).

[4]Iblīs, professing to know the mystery of predetermination (*sirru 'l-qadar*), pleads that it was impossible for him to obey a command which God had eternally willed and decreed that he should disobey. Ḥallāj, while applauding the "self-sacrifice" (*futuwwah*) of Iblīs, at the same time insists on the duty of humble submission to the Divine Commandments.

[5]True lovers of God enjoy the pain their Beloved inflicts on them.

CIII.
LOVE AND LOGIC[1]

Learn from thy Father! He, not falsely proud,
With tears of sorrow all his sin avowed.[2]
Wilt thou, then, still pretend to be unfree
And clamber up Predestination's tree?—
Like Iblīs and his progeny abhorred,
In argument and battle with their Lord.
The blest initiates *know*: what need to *prove*?
From Satan logic, but from Adam love.

CIV.
THE ONE TRUE LIGHT[1]

The lamps are different, but the Light is the same: it comes from Beyond.

If thou keep looking at the lamp, thou art lost: for thence arises the appearance of number and plurality.

Fix thy gaze upon the Light, and thou art delivered from the dualism inherent in the finite body.

O thou who art the kernel of Existence, the disagreement between Moslem, Zoroastrian and Jew depends on the standpoint.

Some Hindus brought an elephant, which they exhibited in a dark shed.

As seeing it with the eye was impossible, every one felt it with the palm of his hand.

The hand of one fell on its trunk: he said, "This animal is like a water-pipe."

Another touched its ear: to him the creature seemed like a fan.

Another handled its leg and described the elephant as having the shape of a pillar.

Another stroked its back. "Truly," said he, "this elephant resembles a throne."

Had each of them held a lighted candle, there would have been no contradiction in their words.

---

[1]*Math.* IV, 1389.

[2]After his fall from Paradise Adam repented and took the blame on himself (*Qur'ān* VII, 22). It is said that he alighted in Sarandīb (Ceylon) and shed floods of tears which caused every valley to be filled with fragrant plants and spices.

---

[1]*Math.* III, 1259. Religions are many, God is One. The intellect, groping in the dark, cannot form any conception of His nature. Only the clairvoyant eye of the mystic sees Him as He really is.

CV.
THE TWELVE GOSPELS[1]

That enemy of the religion of Jesus drew up twelve scriptures, each of which contradicted the other from beginning to end.

In one he made the path of asceticism and fasting to be the basis of repentance and the condition necessary for conversion.[2]

In one he said: "Asceticism profits naught: in this Way there is no salvation but through munificence."[3]

In one he said: "Both your abstinence and your munificence imply that you associate regard for these objects with Him Who is the Object of your worship.[4]

Excepting trust in God and complete resignation in sorrow and joy, all is a deceit and a snare."

In one he said: "It behoves you to do service to God; the notion of putting trust in Him is suspicious."[5]

In one he said: "The Divine Commandments and Prohibitions are not meant for practice, but only to show our incapacity to fulfil them,

So that we may recognize our weakness and confess the power of the Almighty."[6]

In one he said: "Never mind your weakness: to dwell upon that is an act of ingratitude. Beware!

---

[1]*Math.* I, 463. A fanatical Jewish King resolved to extirpate the Christians. Seeing that many secret adherents of the proscribed faith eluded his vengeance, he took counsel with his vizier, who suggested that the King should accuse him of being a Christian in disguise, mutilate him, and drive him into exile; then he would flee to the Christians, win their confidence, and compass their destruction. This plot was carried out. The vizier gradually brought the Christian community under his supreme rule. When all was ripe, he summoned twelve leaders chosen by himself and handed to each one a scroll, appointing him his successor, which was alleged to contain the true gospel of Christ, though in fact the contents of every scroll were different and irreconcilable. Then he killed himself, leaving the Christians to perish in the bitter fighting that immediately broke out among the twelve claimants to the succession.

Older Moslem versions of the legend identify the "vizier" with St. Paul, and it seems to reflect hostile criticism by Christian theologians who favoured St. Peter. Cf. the pseudo-Clementine "Apocalypse of Peter" (*Bulletin of the John Rylands Library* XV, No. 1, p. 179), where Paul is accused of tampering with the twelve books which contained the profession of faith of each of the twelve Apostles (p. 236).

[2]The doctrines mentioned here and below are Ṣūfīstic, though in some cases their development was influenced by Christian theory and practice.

[3]"Munificence" (*jūd*), *i.e.* charity and generosity of soul as opposed to the externals of asceticism.

[4]*i.e.* every form of self-activity and self-regard is "secret polytheism" (*shirk-i khafī*).

[5]If pushed to its extreme logical consequences, the doctrine of trust in God (*tawakkul*) would be incompatible with religious and social duties which no good Moslem can neglect.

[6]Alluding to the heresy of *jabr*. See Nos. XCVII–XCIX.

Regard your power and know that it was given you by Him who is the Absolute."[7]

In one he said, "Leave them both behind: whatsoever involves sense-perception is an idol."[8]

In one he said: "Do not put out this candle of sense-perception: it lights the way to interior concentration.[9]

If you discard sensation and phantasy too soon, you will have put out the lamp of union at midnight."

In one he said: "Put it out—have no fear—so that you may get perceptions thousandfold in exchange;

For by putting it out the light of the spirit is infinitely increased: by your self-denial your Laylā (Beloved) becomes your Majnūn (lover)."

In one he said: "Seek a master to instruct you: among the qualities derived from ancestors you will not find foresight of the end."[10]

Every religious sect only foresaw the end as they themselves conceived it: consequently they fell captive to error.

To foresee the end is not as easy as hand-weaving; else how would there have been such differences of doctrine?

In one he said: "Be a man, be not a slave to men! Take your own course, do not run about in search of a master!"[11]

In one he said: "All this multiformity is one: whoever sees double is a squint-eyed manikin."

In one he said: "How can a hundred be one? He who thinks so is surely mad."

He had no comprehension of the purity of Jesus: he was not imbued with any tincture of the vat of Jesus,

From which the garment of a hundred dyes would emerge as simple and one-coloured as light.[12]

---

[7]See No. XCVII, note 1, and No. XCIX, note 5.

[8]"An idol," *i.e.* an obstacle to realization of the Divine Unity.

[9]The physical and mental faculties of Man enable him to fulfil the purpose for which he was created: without them he could never attain to perfect knowledge of God. Although they are of this world and cannot accompany him to his goal, yet before closing the eyes of sense and intellect he should make full use of such light as they can give to help him on the way.

[10]"Foresight of the end" (*'āqibat-bīnī*), *i.e.* the mystical "second-sight" and universal gnosis reserved for those who have been initiated by a Ṣūfī Pīr. Others regard their own particular forms of belief as final.

[11]"Be a man," *i.e.* a holy man: prophets and saints are "the men" (*mardān*) *par excellence*. See No. XXVIII, note 3.

[12]Moslem authors relate that when Jesus, who was apprenticed to a dyer, cast many-coloured garments into the vat they came out white as snow. This is a parable of the heart of the Perfect Man, which purifies and unifies all that comes into touch with it.

CVI.
THE SHEPHERD'S PRAYER[1]

Moses saw a shepherd on the way, crying, "O Lord Who choosest as Thou wilt,
Where art Thou, that I may serve Thee and sew Thy shoon and comb Thy hair?
That I may wash Thy clothes and kill Thy lice and bring milk to Thee, O worshipful One;
That I may kiss Thy little hand and rub Thy little feet and sweep Thy little room at bed-time."
On hearing these foolish words, Moses said, "Man, to whom are you speaking?
What babble! What blasphemy and raving! Stuff some cotton into your mouth!
Truly the friendship of a fool is enmity: the High God is not in want of suchlike service."
The shepherd rent his garment, heaved a sigh, and took his way to the wilderness.

Then came to Moses a Revelation: "Thou hast parted My servant from Me.
Wert thou sent as a prophet to unite, or wert thou sent to sever?
I have bestowed on every one a particular mode of worship, I have given every one a peculiar form of expression.
The idiom of Hindustān is excellent for Hindūs; the idiom of Sind is excellent for the people of Sind.
I look not at tongue and speech, I look at the spirit and the inward feeling.
I look into the heart to see whether it be lowly, though the words uttered be not lowly.
Enough of phrases and conceits and metaphors! I want burning, burning: become familiar with that burning!
Light up a fire of love in thy soul, burn all thought and expression away!
O Moses, they that know the conventions are of one sort, they whose souls burn are of another."

The religion of love is apart from all religions. The lovers of God have no religion but God alone.

---

[1]*Math.* II, 1720.

CVII.
A REBUKE TO BIGOTS[1]

On this wise did the Jew tell his dream. Oh, there is many a Jew whose end was praiseworthy.[2]
Do not spurn any infidel, for it may be hoped that he will die a Moslem.
What knowledge have you of the close of his life, that you should once and for all avert your face from him?

CVIII.
RELIGIOUS CONTROVERSY[1]

These two-and-seventy sects will remain till the Resurrection: the heretic's talk and argument will not fail.[2]
The number of locks upon a treasure are the proof of its high value.
The long windings of the way, its mountain-passes, and the brigands infesting it, announce the greatness of the traveller's goal.
Every false doctrine resembles a mountain-pass, a precipice, and a brigand.
The blind religious are in a dilemma, for the champions on either side stand firm: each party is delighted with its own path.
Love alone can end their quarrel, Love alone comes to the rescue when you cry for help against their arguments.
Eloquence is dumbfounded by Love: it dare not engage in altercation.
The lover fears to answer back, lest the mystic pearl drop from his mouth.
'Tis as though a marvellous bird perched on your head, and your soul trembled for fear of its flitting:[3]
You dare not move or breathe, you suppress a cough, lest the phoenix should fly away;

---

[1]*Math.* VI, 2450.
[2]The Jew's "dream" refers to a mystical experience symbolized by the epiphany (*tajallī*) of God in His Glory at Mt. Sinai. (*Qur'ān* VI, 139), when "the mountain was shattered and Moses fell down in a swoon."

---

[1]*Math.* V, 3221.
[2]So long as this world lasts, the continuance of false beliefs is necessary and providential: they are formidable obstacles which serve to test the mettle of the "traveller" and must be overcome before he can win the "treasure" that is beyond price.
[3]When the Prophet recited the *Qur'ān*, his Companions (we are told) sat so still and listened so attentively that "one would think birds were perched on their heads." "The sparrow has flown from his head" is an Arabic proverb denoting fluster and perturbation.

And if any one speak, you lay a finger on your lip, meaning, "Hush!"
Love is like that bird: it makes you silent: it puts the lid on the boiling kettle.

CIX.

THE DOCTRINE OF RESERVE[1]

When news arrived of the face of Shamsu'ddīn, the sun in the Fourth Heaven hid itself for shame.[2]
Since his name has come to my life, it behoves me to give some hint of his bounty.
My soul plucks my skirt: she has caught the perfume of Joseph's vest.[3]
She said: "For the sake of our years of companionship, recount one of those sweet ecstasies,
That earth and heaven may laugh with joy, that intellect and spirit and eye may increase a hundredfold."
I said: "Do not lay tasks on me, for I have passed away from myself (*fanā*); my apprehensions are blunted, I know not how to praise.
'Tis unseemly, if one who has not yet returned to consciousness constrain himself to play the braggart.[4]
How should I—not a vein of mine is sensible—describe that Friend Who hath no peer?
The description of this desolate bleeding heart let me leave over till another time."
She answered: "Feed me, for I am hungry, and make haste, for the 'moment' (*waqt*) is a cutting sword.[5]
The Ṣūfī is the son of the 'moment' (*ibnu 'l-waqt*), O comrade: 'tis not the rule of the Way to say 'To-morrow.'[6]
Art not thou a Ṣūfī, then? That which is in hand is reduced to naught by postponing the payment."

---

[1] *Math.* I, 123.

[2] "The face of Shamsu'ddīn," referring to Shams-i Tabrīz and metaphorically to the manifestation (*tajallī*) of God in the Perfect Man.

[3] "My soul," said by the commentators to signify Husamu'ddīn, with whom the poet feels himself mystically one. "The perfume of Joseph's vest," smelt from afar by Jacob (*Qur'ān* XII, 94), describes spiritual rapture.

[4] The Ṣūfī, when really "God-intoxicated," is unconscious of the boastful words that may fall from his lips.

[5] *Waqt*, a technical term for the "moment" of immediate mystical experience, is compared to a sharp sword, because "it cuts the root of the future and the past."

[6] "The son of the moment" should live only in the present, whether he be an adept, whose "moment" is "the eternal Now," or a novice, who must learn that nothing good will come of him if he looks beyond his actual state and hopes to provide for the morrow.

I said to her: "Better that the secret of the Friend should be disguised: do thou hearken to it as implied in the contents of the tale.
Better that the lovers' secret should be told (allegorically) in the talk of others."[7]
She said: "Tell it forth openly and nakedly and without unfaithfulness: do not put me off, O trifler!
Lift the veil and speak nakedly. I do not wear a shirt when I sleep with the Adored One."
I said: "If He should become naked in thy vision, neither wilt thou endure nor thy bosom nor thy waist.
Ask thy wish, but ask with measure: a blade of straw cannot support a mountain.
If the Sun, by whom this world is illumined, approach a little nearer, all will be burned up.
Do not seek trouble and turmoil and bloodshed: say no more concerning the Sun of Tabrīz!"

CX.
UNKNOWING[1]

Lo, for I to myself am unknown, now in God's name what must I do?
I adore not the Cross nor the Crescent, I am not a Giaour nor a Jew.
East nor West, land nor sea, is my home; I have kin nor with angel nor gnome;
I am wrought not of fire nor of foam, I am shaped not of dust nor of dew.
I was born not in China afar, not in Saqsīn and not in Bulghār;
Not in India, where five rivers are, nor 'Irāq nor Khorāsān I grew.
Not in this world nor that world I dwell, not in Paradise neither in Hell;
Not from Eden and Riẓwān I fell, not from Adam my lineage I drew.[2]
In a place beyond uttermost place, in a tract without shadow or trace,
Soul and body transcending I live in the Soul of my Loved One anew!

---

[7]Even to the elect, the mysteries of gnosis can only be communicated—for "he who knows God is dumb"—through a screen of symbolism; and elsewhere Rūmī shows that he, like every Ṣūfī Shaykh, is well aware of the danger of any attempt to divulge them to outsiders.

---

[1]*Dīwān*, *SP*. XXXI.
[2]Riẓwān, the Angel who keeps the keys of Paradise.

CXI.
THE UNITIVE STATE[1]

I am not a congener of the King—far be it from Him!—but I have light from His radiance.[2]
Homogeneity is not in respect of form and essence: water becomes homogeneous with earth in the plant.
Since my *genus* is not the *genus* of my King, my ego passed away (*fanā*) for the sake of His Ego.
My ego passed away, He remains alone: I roll like dust under His horse's feet.
The individual self became dust: the only trace of it is the print of His feet upon its dust.[3]
Become dust at His feet for the sake of that footprint and be as the diadem on the head of an Emperor!

CXII.
THE LIFE EVERLASTING[1]

All human faculties are impermanent: they are naughted on the Day of Resurrection;
Yet the light of the senses and spirits of our fathers is not wholly perishable, like the grass.
Those who have passed from the world are not non-existent: they are steeped in the Divine Attributes.
All their attributes are absorbed in the Attributes of God, even as stars vanish in the presence of the sun.
If you demand authority from the *Qur'ān*, recite the text, "*All of them shall be brought into Our Presence* (*muḥḍarūn*)."[2]

---

[1]*Math.* II, 1170.
[2]Rūmī distinguishes (*Math.* V, 2038) "becoming one with the Light of God" (*ittiḥād-i Nūr*) from "infusion" or "incarnation" (*ḥulūl*), which involves homogeneity. God is Unique. The Perfect Man, though invested with all the Divine Attributes, is not God absolutely: he is real (*ḥaqq*), but not *the* Real (*al-Ḥaqq*). So the Logos of Philo is *θεός*, but not *ὁ θεός* (Bigg, *Christian Platonists of Alexandria*, 2nd ed., p. 42, note 2).
[3]The Perfect Man "bears the mark of God's feet on his dust," *i.e.* the eternal imprint of the Divine Attributes which were stamped upon him before he emerged from potentiality into actual existence; for "he is to the universe what the bezel is to the seal—the bezel whereon is graven the signature that the King seals on His treasures" (Ibnu'l-'Arabī, *Fuṣūṣ*, 13).

---

[1]*Math.* IV, 431.
[2]*Qur'ān* XXXVI, 32 and 53. At the Resurrection all mankind shall be assembled in the presence of God. Rūmī, of course, applies this text to the mystical death (*fanā*) which is life without end (*baqā*).

The person denoted by the word *muḥḍarūn* is not non-existent. Meditate on this, so that you may gain certain knowledge of the everlasting life of the spirit.
The spirit debarred from everlasting life is in torment; the spirit everlastingly united with God is free from barriers.

CXIII.
DOES PERSONALITY SURVIVE?[1]

There is no dervish in the world; and if there be, that dervish is really non-existent.[2]
He exists in respect of the survival of his essence, but his attributes are extinguished in the Attributes of God.[3]
Like the flame of a candle in the presence of the sun, he is really non-existent, though he exists in formal calculation.
The flame's essence is existent in so far as if you put cotton upon it, the cotton will be consumed;
But in reality it is non-existent: it gives you no light, the sun has naughted it.
When an ounce of vinegar is dissolved in a hundred maunds of sugar
The acid flavour is non-existent when you taste the sugar, albeit the ounce exists as a surplus when you weigh.
In the presence of a lion the deer becomes senseless: her existence is but a veil for his.
Analogies drawn by imperfect men concerning the action of the Lord are like the emotion of love, they are not irreverent.

---

[1]*Math.* III, 3669. The term *fanā* is used by Ṣūfīs in connexion with different theories as to the nature of mystical union and may imply:

(1) that the *essence* of the creature (*dhāt-i 'abd*) passed away (*fānī shavad*) in the Essence of God and ceases to exist, just as a drop of water loses its individuality (*ta'ayyun*) in the ocean;

(2) that the *attributes* of the creature (*ṣifāt-i 'abd*) pass away in the Attributes of God: his human attributes are changed (*mubaddal*) into Divine Attributes, so that God becomes his ear and eye;

(3) that the *essence* of the creature vanishes in the Light of the Divine Essence, like the disappearance of stars in the light of the sun. His creatureliness (*khalqiyyah*) does not cease to exist, but is concealed (*makhfī*) under the aspect of Creativeness (*Ḥaqqiyyah*): the Lord (*Rabb*) is manifest, the slave (*'abd*) invisible.

[2]Here "dervish" stands for the perfect type of spiritual poverty, the saint who is denuded of self and dead to the world, even if he appears to live in it.

[3]Nominally he exists, for his "person" (*dhāt-i bashariyyah*) is not annihilated; but since it has been transfigured and "deified," he is really non-existent as an individual and only survives (*bāqī hast*) in virtue of the Divine Life and Energy which constitute his whole being.

The lover's pulse bounds up unabashed, he levels himself with the King.
He appears irreverent, for his claim of love involves equality with the Beloved;
But look deeper: what does he claim? Both he and his claim are naughted in the presence of that Sultan.
*Māta Zayd*ᵘⁿ (Zayd died): if Zayd is the agent (grammatical subject), yet he is not the agent, since he is defunct.
He is the agent only in respect of the grammatical expression; otherwise he is the one acted upon, and Death is his slayer.
What ability to act remains in one who has been so overpowered that all the qualities of an agent are gone from him?

CXIV.
THE SOUL OF THE WORLD[1]

I have circled awhile with the nine Fathers in each Heaven.[2]
For years I have revolved with the stars in their signs.
I was invisible awhile, I was dwelling with Him.
I was in the Kingdom of "*or nearer*," I saw what I have seen.[3]
I receive my nourishment from God, as a child in the womb;
Man is born once, I have been born many times.[4]
Clothed in a bodily mantle, I have busied myself with affairs,
And often have I rent the mantle with my own hands.
I have passed nights with ascetics in the monastery,
I have slept with infidels before the idols in the pagoda.
I am the pangs of the jealous, I am the pain of the sick.
I am both cloud and rain: I have rained on the meadows.
Never did the dust of mortality settle on my skirt, O dervish!

---

[1]*Dīwān*, *SP*, 331. A description of the Perfect Man as the Universal Spirit.
[2]"The nine Fathers": each of the nine celestial spheres was supposed to have a ruling Intelligence, and these spiritual powers are called "Fathers" here. "The *seven* Fathers" is a phrase commonly applied to the planets; some raise the number to nine by adding the Head and Tail of the "Dragon" of astrology (note on *Math*. I, 3991), but such an explanation is hardly satisfying.
[3]Cf. *Qur'ān* LIII, 8–10: "then he approached and descended and was at a distance of two bow-lengths or nearer"—a passage which is generally interpreted as the climax of the Prophet's ascension.
[4]"Man is born once," a hard saying for some modern writers who foist upon Rūmī the Indian doctrine of re-birth. Only the mystic "is born many times," and his experience of birth, death and resurrection belongs to quite a different order of ideas: in reality it typifies the movement of the World-Spirit, with which he is one, evolving through lower forms of soul-life and manifesting itself finally and completely in the Perfect Man. Cf. Nos. LXXXVIII and CXVIII.

I have gathered a wealth of roses in the garden of Eternity.
I am not of water nor fire, I am not of the froward wind,
I am not of moulded clay: I have mocked at them all.
O son, I am not Shams-i Tabrīz, I am the pure Light.
If thou seest me, beware! Tell not any one what thou hast seen!

CXV.
DEIFICATION[1]

When a fly is plunged in honey, all the members of its body are reduced to the same condition, and it does not move. Similarly the term *istighrāq* (absorption in God) is applied to one who has no conscious existence or initiative or movement. Any action that proceeds from him is not his own. If he is still struggling in the water, or if he cries out, "Oh, I am drowning," he is not said to be in the state of absorption. This is what is signified by the words *Ana 'l-Ḥaqq* "I am God." People imagine that it is a presumptuous claim, whereas it is really a presumptuous claim to say *Ana 'l-'abd* "I am the slave of God"; and *Ana 'l-Ḥaqq* "I am God" is an expression of great humility. The man who says *Ana 'l-'abd* "I am the slave of God" affirms two existences, his own and God's, but he that says *Ana 'l-Ḥaqq* "I am God" has made himself non-existent and has given himself up and says "I am God," *i.e.* "I am naught, He is all: there is no being but God's." This is the extreme of humility and self-abasement.

CXVI.
THE GOD-MAN[1]

To praise and glorify him is to glorify God: Divine fruit is growing from the essential nature of this tray.
Apples grow from this basket in fine variety: 'tis no harm if you bestow on it the name of "tree."

---

[1]*Fīhi mā fīhi*, 49. See No. LXXXVIII, note 5, and cf. *Math.* II, 1346: When he (the mystic) falls into the dyeing-vat of *Hū* (the Absolute God), and you say to him, "Arise," he cries in rapture, "I am the vat: do not blame me." That "I am the vat" is the same as saying "I am God" (*ana 'l-Ḥaqq*): he has the colour of fire, albeit he is iron.

The colour of the iron is naughted in the colour of the fire: the iron boasts of its fierceness, though actually it is silent.
It has become glorified by the colour and nature of the fire: it says, "I am the fire, I am the fire."

---

[1]*Math.* VI, 3204. In this analogy "the Apple-tree" is God, and the Perfect Man is likened to a tray or basket of apples, *i.e.* Divine Attributes, which provide spiritual food for all who believe in him.

Call this basket "the Apple-tree," for between the two there is a secret union.
Deem this basket to be the Tree of Fortune and sit happily beneath its shade.

CXVII.
THE SPIRITUAL ASCENSION[1]

If you join the ranks of those who make the Ascension, not-being will bear you aloft like Burāq.[2]
'Tis not like the ascension of a mortal to the moon; nay, but like the ascension of a sugar-cane to sugar.
'Tis not like the ascension of a vapour to the sky; nay, but like the ascension of an embryo to rationality.

CXVIII.
THE PROGRESS OF MAN[1]

First he appeared in the realm inanimate;
Thence came into the world of plants and lived
The plant-life many a year, nor called to mind
What he had been; then took the onward way
To animal existence, and once more

[1]*Math.* IV, 552.
[2]"Not-being," *i.e.* the passing away (*fanā*) of self-consciousness. Burāq is the steed on which the Prophet is said to have ridden to Heaven.

[1]*Math.* IV, 3637. The doctrine of soul-development set forth by Rūmī in this and other passages, *e.g.* Nos. V (note 2), XLII (note 3), LXI and LXV, is not peculiar to him: it appears in Moslem philosophy and mysticism at a much earlier date and is founded on Aristotle's theory of the triple nature of the soul as poetically described by Milton (*Paradise Lost* V, 479 *seqq.*):

So from the root
Springs lighter the green stalk, from thence the leaves
More aery, last the bright consummate flower
Spirits odorous breathes: flowers and their fruit,
Man's nourishment, by gradual scale sublimed,
To vital spirits aspire, to animal,
To intellectual; give both life and sense,
Fancy and understanding; whence the Soul
Reason receives, and Reason is her being.

To complete the parallel, these lines should be read in connexion with Milton's treatise *De doctrinâ Christianâ*, where he elaborates the view that "all creation, inanimate and animate, consists but of diverse forms or degrees of one and the same original or prime *matter*; which *matter* was originally an efflux or emanation out of the very substance of the One Eternal Spirit" (Masson, *The Poetical Works of John Milton*, III, 361).

Remembers naught of that life vegetive.
Save when he feels himself moved with desire
Towards it in the season of sweet flowers,
As babes that seek the breast and know not why.[2]
Again the wise Creator whom thou knowest
Uplifted him from animality
To Man's estate; and so from realm to realm
Advancing, he became intelligent,
Cunning and keen of wit, as he is now.
No memory of his past abides with him,
And from his present soul he shall be changed.

Though he is fallen asleep, God will not leave him
In this forgetfulness. Awakened, he
Will laugh to think what troublous dreams he had,
And wonder how his happy state of being
He could forget and not perceive that all
Those pains and sorrows were the effect of sleep
And guile and vain illusion. So this world
Seems lasting, though 'tis but the sleeper's dream;
Who, when the appointed Day shall dawn, escapes
From dark imaginings that haunted him,
And turns with laughter on his phantom griefs
When he beholds his everlasting home.

CXIX.
"RIPENESS IS ALL"[1]

Since thou canst not bear the unveiled Light, drink the Word of Wisdom, for its light is veiled,[2]
To the end that thou mayst become able to receive the Light, and behold without veils that which now is hidden,
And traverse the sky like a star; nay, journey unconditioned, without a sky.

---

[2]The functions of the vegetive soul are growth, assimilation, and reproduction. Spring flowers and verdure awaken in the animal soul, which is the "child" of the vegetive soul, subconscious memories of its "mother."

---

[1]*Math.* III, 1286.
[2]By devoting himself to his Shaykh and absorbing spiritual truth in the form of words the disciple is gradually prepared for entrance, if God will, into the illuminative and contemplative life.

'Twas thus thou camest into being from non-existence. How didst thou come? Thou camest insensibly.[3]

The ways of thy coming thou rememberest not, but I will give thee an indication.

Let thy mind go, then be mindful! Close thine ear, then listen!

Nay, I will not tell, for thou art still unripe: thou art in thy springtime, thou hast not seen the summer.

This world is as the tree: we are like the half-ripened fruit upon it.

The unripe fruits cling fast to the bough, because they are not fit for the palace;

But when they have ripened and become sweet and delicious—after that, they lose hold of the bough.

Even so does the kingdom of the world lose its savour for him whose mouth has been sweetened by the great felicity.

Something remains untold, but the Holy Spirit will tell thee without me as the medium.

Nay, thou wilt tell it to thine own ear—neither I nor another, O thou who art one with me—

Just as, when thou fallest asleep, thou goest from the presence of thyself into the presence of thyself

And hearest from thyself that which thou thinkest is told thee secretly by some one in the dream.[4]

O good friend, thou art not a single "thou": thou art the sky and the deep sea.

Thy mighty infinite "Thou" is the ocean wherein myriads of "thou's" are sunken.

Do not speak, so that thou mayst hear from the Speakers what cannot be uttered or described.

Do not speak, so that the Spirit may speak for thee: in the ark of Noah leave off swimming!

---

[3]"From non-existence," *i.e.* from the unobjectified world of Unity. See No. LXIV and No. V.

[4]The mysteries revealed in veridical dreams are not really communicated to the dreamer by the apparitions with which he imagines he is conversing. Nothing is external to the soul that knows God to be its true self and sees its descent and ascent as phases of His timeless Self-revelation.